NEW ZEALAND IN YOUR POCKET

NEW ZEALAND
IN YOUR POCKET

A STEP-BY-STEP GUIDE
AND TRAVEL ITINERARY

BY ARNOLD SCHUCHTER

Horizon Books

British Library Cataloguing in Publication Data
Schuchter, Arnold
  New Zealand in your pocket: a step-by-step guide and
  travel itinerary.—(Pocket travellers).
  1. New Zealand—Practical information—For immigrants
  I. Title II. Series
  919.31'0437
  ISBN 1-85461-055-4

© 1988 by Arnold Schuchter
UK edition © 1990 by Horizon Books Ltd
Maps Janice St Marie

This edition first published in 1990 by Horizon Books Ltd,
Plymbridge House, Estover Road, Plymouth PL6 7PZ, United
Kingdom. Tel: Plymouth (0752) 705251. Telex: 45635. Fax: (0752)
777603.

Typeset by Kestrel Data, Exeter
Printed in Great Britain by BPCC Wheatons Ltd, Exeter

CONTENTS

HOW TO USE THIS BOOK

Welcome to the infinite variety that is New Zealand.
Following the do-it-yourself tour described in this book, you
will:

■Acclimatise yourself to Kiwi country by covering the gamut
of urban, coastal, island and mountain 'bush' activities in the
Auckland region, and enjoy delicious meals.

■Tour the glorious Bay of Islands and the giant kauri forests
on the west coast of historic Northland.

■Travel south to Wellington passing through the scenic
Coromandel Peninsula, explore Rotorua-Taupo-Tongariro's
volcanic mountains and trout-filled lakes and rivers, and
maybe jetboat down the beautiful Wanganui River to the
'Garden City' of the same name.

■Cross Cook Strait on the Inter-Island Ferry from
Wellington through the South Island's fabulous Marlborough
Sounds.

■Leave the 'sun belt of the South Island' from the ferry port
of Picton and head down the Kaikoura Coast to the
marvellous variety of attractions in the Christchurch region
and the South Island's most picturesque city.

■Travel from Christchurch over Burke's Pass and past glacial
lakes to Mt. Cook National Park.

■Pass through Mackenzie Country, rimmed by the Southern
Alps, over Lindis Pass to the spectacular mountains, lakes and
rivers of Queenstown, Te Anau, Fiordland National Park and
the world renowned Milford Sound.

■■Drive through the beautiful Wanaka/Mt. Aspiring
National Park region over Haast Pass to the west coast's Fox
and Franz Josef Glaciers.

■Return to Christchurch over Arthur's Pass after exploring
some of the west coast's lakes, as well as greenstone and gold
mining attractions, to complete your tour on beautiful Banks
Peninsula.

For each tour, this book provides:
1. A **Suggested Schedule** of where to go, in what order,
   how long to stay there, what to see and how to travel
   between destinations.
2. The most unique and scenic **Sightseeing Highlights**,
   rated: ●●●'Don't miss'; ●● 'Try hard to see'; and ●
   'Worthwhile if you can make it'.
3. My recommendations for **Where to Eat** and **Where to
   Stay**, in all budget ranges.

4. **Itinerary Options**, activities and side trips, usually
   requiring more time or money.
5. **Maps** of all areas covered in this tour.

Customise your own itinerary. This guide can be followed
literally, or you can select any tour or combination of tours as
your itinerary, or even take only one option in one chapter
and make it your entire holiday. Some travellers want to 'see
it all', while others prefer to concentrate their time in a few
selected areas with a large variety of activities or a single,
unique sporting/outdoor activity such as deep-sea fishing,
diving, white-water rafting, or perhaps just relaxing. Each
tour in this book is modular and, within certain limitations,
can be rearranged to suit your travel style. With the exception
of about five days spent in three cities (Auckland, Wellington
and Christchurch), most sightseeing and activities on both
islands centre on coastlines, mountains, lakes and rivers.

New Zealand in Your Pocket is for the young at heart who
love the outdoors. Seeing the best of New Zealand's diverse
landscapes and coastal waters makes for a very full itinerary.
This book guides you step by step through each area to
experience a full range of the finest this marvellous country
has to offer.

Cost and budget considerations

The prices quoted in this book for accommodation and meals
are for two people travelling together unless otherwise
indicated. All prices are in New Zealand dollars, shown as
NZ$ with approximate sterling equivalents.

New Zealand is not expensive for an extended holiday, as
long as you plan your budget carefully and stick to it. A single
person can expect to spend NZ$40-$50 (£15-£20) a day for a
room, NZ$25-$35 (£10-£13) for meals, NZ$60 (£22) for
daily sightseeing excursions, tours, admission fees, etc., and
NZ$10 (£4) for entertainment and miscellaneous. A couple
will save on the room cost per person but on nothing else—
maybe spending a little more on sightseeing and
entertainment. Two people will spend about £2,900 on this
itinerary plus the cost of getting there. If you hire a car, it
will cost at least NZ$75 (£28) per day plus petrol, or another
NZ$1,650 (about £600). The approximate grand total for the
trip for two persons is £5,000, plus the fare there. This does
not include souvenirs, sheepskin or wool purchases, skiing,
cruising or flightseeing.

An individual budget traveller, staying in youth hostels,
using a Travelpass, watching pennies for meals and choosing

to walk rather than pay for sightseeing excursions, can make the trip for £1,500 or less, depending on the season.

Entry requirements

You need a passport valid for at least three months beyond the date of your expected departure from New Zealand and a return ticket. No visa is required by British citizens. No inoculations are required. Each person over 17 can bring in a quart of spirits, wine or beer, 200 cigarettes, 50 cigars, plus up to NZ$250 (£94) worth of duty-free items. Bring in as much money as you like, and there is no duty on your other personal possessions. Prohibited items include food, plants, animals or animal products, insects, other squirming objects (except children), and drugs other than over-the-counter products and prescriptions.

If you plan to spend at least three weeks in New Zealand, technically you can be asked to prove that you have a certain amount of money with you in cash, travellers' cheques or valid credit cards. I've never experienced this type of welcoming 'investigation' and, chances are, neither will you.

Currency

New Zealand has one, two, five, ten, 20 and 50 dollar notes, and one, two, five, ten, 20, and 50 cent coins. At the time of writing a New Zealand dollar is worth about 40p, but the relative values change daily.

Travellers' cheques can be exchanged for New Zealand currency at any bank without a fee and even earn you a slight premium over exchanging pounds. Trading banks are open from 9:30 a.m. to 4:00 p.m. Monday to Friday, but not on Saturdays or public holidays. American Express, Diners Club, Access and Visa credit cards are welcomed at large and medium-sized hotels, tourist shops and higher-priced restaurants, but you'll enjoy more flexibility with a supply of both Sterling and New Zealand travellers' cheques and, off the beaten path, about NZ$100 in cash.

Seasons, holidays and hours

New Zealand's seasons are the opposite of those in Europe. Spring is September to November; summer, December to February; autumn, March to May; and winter, June to August. The climate is temperate. Seasonal variations are noticeable, but only extreme in the mountains and the far southern part of the South Island. You can gaze at snow on the mountains of both islands from their mild coastlines. Winter on the North Island tends to be wet, but only dismal for a few midwinter days in Auckland. On the South Island, when wet weather hits the mountains, frequently with fierce winds, watch out for rapidly flooding rivers and streams, or blizzards that happen before you can say, 'Let's get out of here!'

In July, the coldest month in Auckland, the average temperature is 58 degrees Fahrenheit. July also has the most days of rain (12), so the dampness (70% humidity) can make it seem colder. January, the warmest month in Auckland, is also one of the driest (6 inches of rainfall) but still humid (64%). Christchurch, a little colder in midwinter (51 degrees) and a little cooler in midsummer (71 degrees), also has high humidity (57–70%).

There are substantial variations throughout each island. It rains twice as much in the Bay of Islands as on the south-east coast south of Gisborne. Most of the north and east coasts of the South Island are drier than the North Island. The west coast can be quite wet and colder than on the east side of the Southern Alps.

Unless you plan to ski, don't travel to New Zealand in the winter. Autumn and especially spring and summer are more beautiful and drier. But in the summer months, when schools break up and New Zealanders are on holiday, accommodation, transport and tourist attractions are scarce and heavily booked, prices go up and you have to scramble and pay more for less.

National and school holidays: For travel planning purposes, the significance of New Zealand's national holidays is that the country shuts down. Don't arrive on one or try to travel anywhere. Stay put. Don't drive if you are low on petrol. Take a walk, sail or whatever you like, purchasing food the day before. Don't bother looking for restaurants or pubs except maybe a stray milk bar in the hinterlands. Be prepared for these holidays:

New Year's Day
Waitangi Day—February 6
Good Friday and Easter Monday
Anzac Day—April 25
Queen's Birthday—first Monday in June
Labour Day—fourth Monday in October
Christmas Day
Boxing Day—December 26

If the holiday falls on a Tuesday, Wednesday or Thursday, it shifts to the previous Monday; on Friday, Saturday or Sunday to the following Monday. Also watch for local holidays in every part of the country, such as January 29 in Auckland and

January 22 in Wellington, which can be equally hazardous to your travel plans.

The main school and family holiday period is from mid-December to the end of January. Schools are also closed for two weeks in May and in the beginning of August.

Shopping times and business hours: Most shops are open from 9:00 a.m. to 5:30 p.m. Monday to Thursday (until 9:00 p.m. on Friday in major cities) and on Saturday until noon. Only tourist shops in season and dairies will be open Sunday. Offices, businesses and post offices are open weekdays from 8:00 a.m. to 5:00 p.m. Banks are open from 10:00 a.m. to 4:00 p.m. Monday to Friday.

What to bring

Be prepared for any kind of weather at any time of year with wet weather gear, a windproof jacket, light and heavier sweaters (which can be purchased in New Zealand) and some medium-weight clothing, shorts, a swimsuit, sunglasses and sun-tan cream (expensive in New Zealand), comfortable walking/hiking shoes and good socks. Men who plan to eat out at an expensive restaurant or visit nightclubs should bring an appropriate jacket, shirt and tie. Women, bring a dress or skirt and blouse. And, of course, bring your 35mm camera with plenty of film.

Flying to New Zealand

Both British Airways and Air New Zealand have direct services from London to Auckland, British Airways from Heathrow and Air New Zealand from Gatwick, and both have three flights a week. Excursion fares vary according to when you travel—from just under £1,000 return in the off-peak season at the time of writing to about £1,400 at the most popular times (September and just before Christmas). Check with your travel agent for up-to-date information.

There are cheaper fares available if you are prepared to 'rough it' a little. Special deals are advertised in the classified columns of the national press, and usually involve changing planes in out-of-the-way places, and sometimes at pretty ungodly hours!

Getting around by car or camper van

Looking at New Zealand on a globe or in an atlas, merely a tiny sliver in the vast South Pacific next to the far larger Australian continent, easily leads to the illusion that North and South Islands can be covered comfortably in a car in a matter of days. Your suspicion that this isn't true will be confirmed quickly. New Zealand has a good network of roads, but they are not motorways. This itinerary is based on an average driving speed of 40 mph or less.

Hired cars normally cost NZ$90–$130 (£36–£50) per day with unlimited mileage. You can save money with a discount package that combines car hire, accommodation and airfare. Your travel agent can give you details.

You may want to consider hiring a camper van and save additional money by staying in caravan parks. The savings on accommodation, however, can be offset by higher petrol consumption.

Immediately learn the 'right hand rule': always give way to traffic approaching on your right except for a car directly in front that intends to turn right. The maximum speed limit is 100 kmh (roughly 60 mph), or 50 kmh (30 mph) in built-up areas. An 'L.S.Z.' (Limited Speed Zone) sign means no speed limit—use your good judgment.

Don't drink when driving! New Zealand laws are even tougher than those in the U.K. Watch out for sheep and cows, school buses and children. Keep your petrol tank full, use chains when required, don't try to drive across flooding rivers, and have a safe and enjoyable trip.

By coach and train

Hiring a car or camper van is extremely helpful but not necessary in order to tour New Zealand using this guide.

The New Zealand Railway Road Services (NZRR) provides a coach, train and ferry service around the country. There are three **Travelpass** discount packages: eight-day, 15-day and 22-day. Prices vary according to season, but Travelpasses deserve serious consideration for part or all of your trip. Travelpasses must usually be purchased before you leave home. From 15 December to 31 January, however, all three passes have to be purchased in New Zealand. Each pass is undated; starting on the day you begin travel on the NZRR system, use is on a consecutive day basis. Additional days (up to six) can be bought. Using these passes you can travel anywhere by coach, train and the inter-island ferry from Wellington to Picton for less than NZ$23 (£9) per day, whereas full-day bus travel alone otherwise can cost NZ$20–$50 (£8–£20). The Travelpass also provides discounts at Best Western Motels.

Also, ask your travel agent about current prices on seven-day, 10-day and 15-day **Kiwi Coach Passes** jointly offered by NZRR, Mount Cook Line and Newmans Coachlines, which get you everywhere you want to go for about NZ$15 (£6) per day. You must purchase the pass before leaving home.

By air

Four major carriers—Air New Zealand, Mount Cook Airlines, Newmans Airways and Ansett Airlines (the competitive newcomer)—provide ample air services between all major towns and tourist centres, supplemented by numerous smaller airlines. The major airlines offer special deals on domestic flights, so consult your travel agent for details.

Where to stay

New Zealand offers an outstanding variety of accommodation at reasonable prices, especially for foreign currency. Carry cash or travellers' cheques and don't depend on credit cards unless you're following the hotel/motel chain circuit. You can wait until you arrive in New Zealand to make reservations except in peak summer (including Christmas and January) and Easter, at ski resorts in prime winter months, or at the top lodges.

If you're driving, the best accommodation value in many parts of New Zealand is farm holidays (NZ$90–$140 (£36–£56) double per night with breakfast and dinner) and non-farm 'home-hosting' (NZ$60 (£24) double B&B or NZ$60–$70 (£24–£28) per person including all meals). Pick the type of farm you wish to visit (sheep, dairying, cattle, cropping or high country), and share meals with the hosts. Take part in farm activities if you wish. Reservations, which are essential, can be made through your travel agent or direct. Contact:

Farm Holidays Ltd., P.O. Box 1436, Wellington, tel. 723-2126;

Farmhouse Holidays, Kitchener Rd., Milford, Auckland, tel. 492-171;

New Zealand Farm Holidays, Private Bag, Parnell, Auckland, tel. 394-780;

Farm Home and Country Home Holidays, Box 31-250, Auckland, tel. 492-171;

Home Stay/Farm Stay, P.O. Box 630, Rotorua, tel. 24-895, including non-farm homes throughout the North Island.

Town and Country Home Hosting, Box 143, Cambridge, tel. 27-6511;

Rural Tours, P.O. Box 228, Cambridge, tel. 07-127;

Rural Holidays New Zealand, P.O. Box 2155, Christchurch, tel. 61-919;

Friendly Kiwi Home Hosting Service, P.O. Box 5049, Port Nelson, tel. 85-575;

N.Z. Home Hospitality, P.O. Box 309, Nelson, tel. 84-727, also offering non-farm stays throughout both islands; and

New Zealand Travel Hosts, 279 Williams St., Kaiapoi, tel. 6340, for home hosting.

Get a copy of the *New Zealand Accommodation Guide* from the NZTP office in Auckland for a list of individual farms and home hosts.

Motel flats/tourist flats (complete apartments) usually include two bedrooms, a living room, a fully equipped kitchen, and a bathroom with shower for NZ$35–$49 (£14–£19) double (low-price), with a pool and spa on the premises. Medium-priced motels cost NZ$50–$69 (£20–£27). Serviced motels—rather Spartan motel rooms—cost slightly less than tourist flats.

An economical way to book hotels is as part of an airline package that also includes a hired car and a quality hotel for a fixed price. Check with your travel agent for details.

Bed-and-breakfast guesthouses and small hotels provide lodging and breakfast for under NZ$60 (£24) double. The hospitality and helpfulness are typically wonderful, and the other guests are the kind of New Zealanders and visitors you want to meet. Depending on the locality and season, booking may be difficult. One of the advantages of following this itinerary is that you can book ahead and be assured of getting the ones you want.

Campsites, with communal bathroom, laundry and kitchen facilities, are terrific value. They offer tent and caravan sites from NZ$4–$7 (£1.60–£2.80) per person, a few cabins or A-frames from NZ$15–$28 (£6–£11) double (provide your own sleeping bag), on-site caravans from about NZ$15 (£6) single or double, and sometimes flats from about NZ$28 (£11) for two or three persons (no linen). If you're an AA member, which I advise for drivers, call in at any AA office for their *Accommodation, Camping and Breakdown Guide to the South Island, Accommodation and Camping Guide South Island, AA North Island Outdoor Guide, New Zealand Holiday Parks Guide to N.Z. Camp Caravan and Cabin Accommodation*, and the directory of the Camp & Cabin Association.

Youth hostels, everything from farmhouses to modern buildings, are in excellent locations throughout the country. 'Youth' can include anyone over five years old with a membership, which you can purchase either before you leave home or in New Zealand. Additional advantages of membership include discounts on car hire, rail and ferry fares, ski packages and other outdoor activities, and tour packages with YHA accommodation and transport. Contact **Australia House**, 36 Customs St. East, Auckland to find out about current membership benefits.

All youth hostel prices quoted in the book are for 'Seniors' (over 18). With your sleeping bag and pillowcase, bunk beds are available in dormitories sharing communal facilities, priced from NZ$9 to NZ$12 (£4–£5) per person. The maximum stay is three nights, facilities are closed during the day, curfew time usually is 10:30 p.m. except in major cities, and help with cleaning up is expected. Book in advance during school holiday periods, especially in popular tourist areas. Send a money order for the first night, along with an international reply coupon, to National Reservations Centre, P.O. Box 436, Christchurch. A **Wanderlust Pass** for discounts can be obtained from YHA offices in Auckland, Wellington and Christchurch together with a handbook to New Zealand's Hostels.

YMCAs and YWCAs are a very attractive budget option in major cities and towns, starting at about NZ$19 (£8) per person with breakfast and dinner. Although many students live in them, these facilities are frequently less crowded, even during peak season, and offer more privacy, with some single or shared rooms.

At the other end of the budget spectrum are luxury and first-class hotels, many operated by international hotel chains, and sporting lodges that offer unique facilities and experiences for fishing and shooting enthusiasts. Book hotel reservations at the time you make international air reservations in order to obtain discount packages or discounts offered by the airlines. Superior and luxury-class hotels in New Zealand are usually easy to find and book through their British sales centres. The best are the Tourist Hotel Corporation of New Zealand's uniquely located, one-of-a-kind facilities (THC, 35 Albert St., Auckland, tel. 773-689).

Many modern, high-standard hotels and motor inns in all major and secondary tourist areas cost NZ$70–$100 (£28–£40) single. The NZTP or DAA offices will gladly book them for you after your arrival in Auckland. The same is true for all of my recommended accommodation, which starts at NZ$70 (£28) and goes downward.

Where and what to eat

The New Zealand eating experience that should not be missed is a Maori *hangi* (feast) in Rotorua, which features many steamed dishes and Maori entertainment.

Surprisingly few restaurants do justice to the quality of
New Zealand meat or seafood. In or out of restaurants, the
foods to look for are: roast spring lamb (especially October-
January), steaks and roast beef, farm-raised venison, tasty and
inexpensive meat and savoury pies (egg and bacon, mince),
and great seafood—five varieties of blue cod, fresh plump
bluff oysters in the winter and small sweet Auckland rock
oysters, Marlborough scallops in spring and summer, crayfish,
marinated mussels year-round, smoked and fresh salmon,
John Dory, orange roughy, grouper, kingfish, flounder,
snapper and squid. Look for melons in summer, kiwi fruit in
winter and spring, fresh vegetables and all kinds of berries.

Though New Zealand is not on the international gourmet
tour circuit, French-New Zealand or French provincial
cuisine in and near the major cities is quite respectable and, in
some instances, outstanding.

Stay at a bed-and-breakfast and the quantity of good food
may even carry you until dinner. Otherwise wait until coffee
time to have a snack with your coffee. For lunch I
recommend eating places in each city and town for light
lunches (about NZ$5–$7 (£2–£3)), but look carefully at each
day's schedule to see if an economical picnic lunch at a park
or beach from a local delicatessen wouldn't be more fun.
Tourist spots are full of pubs and take-aways, and every town
of any size has its Cobb & Co. with reasonable prices. Many
of the best dinner spots are unpretentious BYOs (bring your
own wine). Most expensive restaurants are licensed to serve
alcohol, except on Sundays, and you are expected to dress up.
You don't have to tip anywhere, but if the service is good, a
tip is appreciated.

Information sources

Information to supplement this book is available from the
New Zealand Tourist Office at New Zealand House,
Haymarket, London SW1Y 4TQ.

New Zealand Travel Offices, providing information and
complete travel services, are located in:

     Auckland (tel. 09-798-180)
     Rotorua (tel. 073-85-179)
     Wellington (tel. 04-739-269)
     Christchurch (tel. 03-794-900)
     Dunedin (tel. 024-740-344)
     Queenstown (tel. 143/379)

Every city and larger town has a public relations office (PRO)
and visitors' information centre.

NEW ZEALAND IS UNIQUE

Flora and fauna

When New Zealand broke away from Australia and Antarctica, about 70 million years ago, its geographical isolation ensured a unique assortment of animal and plant life not found elsewhere. Dense forest with 112 native tree species and thick undergrowth supported 250 species of native birds, many flightless, that grazing animals and predators introduced by settlers reduced dramatically. Many of the species released by European settlers, like cats, weasels, deer, opossums, pigs and hares, live in Urewera National Park, the North Island's largest forest.

The most famous survivor is the flightless, nocturnal kiwi, New Zealand's national emblem, named after its piercing whistle, 'keee-weee'. You're more likely to hear than see the kiwi in the bush, especially in the middle of the night, so look for it in nocturnal houses such as the one at Auckland's zoo. The kiwi is only one of several remaining flightless birds, including the kakapo, kea, waka and the very rare blue and iridescent green takahe, thought to be extinct until a colony was rediscovered in Fiordland, where all of these birds live, along with the rare southern crested grebe and the Fiordland crested penguin.

At lower elevations, you'll find New Zealand's version of pampas grass, toe toe, along with rimu, northern rate and tawa forest, fading to beech, totara and tawari above 2,600 feet. This vegetation shelters three species of parrot—kaka, morepork and red-crowned and yellow-crowned parakeet—and the white-breasted kereru, New Zealand's only native pigeon, easily sighted here or in Tongariro National Park because it makes a loud flapping noise when it flies. From north to south there are many different birds, but always abundant.

In each of the mountain areas you'll visit on the North and South Islands, variations in climate (wet side and dry side) and altitude produce distinctive vegetation zones. In Tongariro National Park (Tour 9), Urewera National Park and Egmont National Park on the North Island, and the Southern Alps from Arthur's Pass National Park to Fiordland National Park, a green canopy of broadleaf rainforests, with thick undergrowth, yields through several different forest zones to shrub, tussock and alpine herb zones, sprinkled with buttercups and daisies, before only lichen can survive below permanent snowlines.

There are more than 150 species of ferns in New Zealand, growing everywhere together with mostly white or cream-coloured flowers, including 60 species of orchids. Stewart Island alone has 30 species and a wealth of other native plants and rare birds like kakas, Stewart Island robins, Stewart Island brown kiwis, fernbirds, plied shags, Stewart Island shags, yellow-eyed penguins and the kakapo, also found in Fiordland.

About 500 species of alpine flowers are found only in New Zealand. Above the 3,000-foot level, the tiny green rifleman and silver eye inhabit the beeches, safely below the sub-alpine tussock shrublands minutely searched for small birds and animals by native falcons. In December and January, birds of Tongariro's tussockland fly over vast acreages of alpine flora blooming white with touches of purple or mauve orchids. In December you'll see the pohutukawa (New Zealand Christmas Tree) bloom, and in spring the parasitic rata's red blossoms and the bright yellow Kowhai blossoms. Aging gnarled pohutukawas form the backdrop of Auckland's sandy bays tucked between headlands on the eastern shoreline.

New Zealand's native kauri is a conifer, botanically in the pine and fir family of less magnificent trees found in Australia, Malaysia and Pacific Islands. The kauri's lower branches and bark shed leaving a massive crown of leathery leaves as high as 150 feet above the large mound of humus covering its root system.

No discussion of New Zealand's flora and fauna would be complete without mentioning the islands' most common mammals—sheep. More than 70 million sheep dot the countryside, about 20 for every New Zealander. New Zealand is the third largest producer and the second largest exporter of wool in the world. Sheep are raised for wool in the hill country, with lamb and mutton production in the low country. In 1850-80, while Maori tribes and the government on the North Island were at war over land, huge tracts of the South Island's tussockland were rapidly being occupied by Australian Merino sheep farmers. Sheep scab disease, a plague of rabbits and the discovery of gold in the 1860s slowed the expansion of sheep grazing. But the introduction of refrigeration and refrigerated cargo ships in the early 1880s spurred lamb-breeding for overseas meat consumers.

At the Agrodome in Rotorua, the sheep station in Queenstown, and other locations, sheep herders put talented sheep dogs through their paces with vocal and whistle commands. Professional sheep-shearers show how it's done.

New Zealand's volcanic legacy

Volcanoes dominate the Auckland-Coromandel Peninsula landscape from air, sea and land. The symmetrical Rangitoto Island, guarding the entrance to Auckland's Waitemata Harbour, erupted a mere 200 years ago. Auckland itself is situated on a plateau marked by 60 volcanic cones around which early Maori settlements clustered for defence. The volcanic ramparts of the Waitakeres rise to the west, descending to black sandy beaches on the western shores pounded by Tasman breakers. Today these are parks and reserves among the best viewpoints. The Coromandel Ranges are volcanic stumps rising steeply east of the Firth of Thames. Volcanic remnants still exist, and on Tour 6 you'll dig hot water pools around Hot Water Beach.

Polynesian voyagers from 'Hawaiki' landed their canoe, *Te Awara*, at Maketu (south of what is today Tauranga—Tour 7) on the Bay of Plenty in the middle of the 14th century. According to legend, Ngatoroirangi travelled south to Tongariro and, when close to freezing to death in a snowstorm, called on his sisters in Hawaiki to bring warmth. His route south is marked by geothermal activity, from the active volcano Whakaari (White Island) through the geysers, steaming cliffs, bubbling pools of mud and hot springs spurting from the ground around Rotorua and Lake Taupo, to the active volcanoes of Tongariro National Park. The Maoris had been using the healing properties of local mineral hot pools, the 'healing springs', 500 years before tourists were first drawn to Rotorua's thermal wonders, especially the Pink and White Terraces of Lake Rotomahana, produced by hydrothermal changes in the pumice, and destroyed by the eruption of Tarawera in 1886.

Maori art, crafts and settlements

The earliest history of New Zealand is linked to ancestors of the Maoris from eastern Polynesia. Maori mythology has Kupe discovering Aotearoa in about 950 AD followed about four hundred years later by the armada of canoes to which Maori tribes trace their genealogies. Archaeological remains suggest that as early as 1000 AD Maori hunters of huge, now-extinct flightless birds (moas) roamed the coastal South Island. The giant moa offered plentiful food and forests yielded huge trees (kauri) for carving dugout canoes and constructing dwellings. Later, as the moas became rare, tribal and sub-tribal groups settled in villages.

Pas are fortified settlements built by a large family or part

of a tribe, housing the local chief and his warband and also
serving as a dwelling place, a food store, a centre for
craftsmen and a refuge against attack. Located on a defensible
high point, a coastal headland or the edge of a swamp, the *pa*
and its surroundings were fortified with earthworks, scarping
on the sides and ditches, with living quarters on artificial
terraces. *Pas* were built and used from the late 15th or early
16th centuries to the early 1800s. *Pas* can be seen in the Bay
of Islands, Kerikeri, Russell, the Auckland isthmus, the Bay
of Plenty, Waikato, Taranaki (southwest) and Hawke's Bay
(southeast) on the North Island.

The years that followed European settlement saw the
construction of communal meeting houses (*whare whakairo*)
for social purposes and to discuss many problems: fighting
with settlers, British, and other tribes; land problems; disease;
guns, and so forth. These meeting houses are highly
ornamented displays of Maori wood-carving skills. See for
example: the Tama-te Kapua at Ohinemutu, in Rotorua;
Poho-o Rawiri, the largest meeting house in New Zealand,
near Gisborne; Te Hauki Turanga in the National Museum
(originally built in Poverty Bay); Hotunui in the Auckland
Museum; and the Waitangi Treaty House on the Waitangi
Peninsula.

The greenstone rocks that you can see in Auckland and
Hokitika's factories on the South Island's west coast are only
found in New Zealand in the Arahura and Taramakau
riverbeds flowing from the Southern Alps to the Tasman Sea.
Greenstone was so revered by Maori tribes for tools,
ornaments and weapons that they trekked over the Alps to the
west coast to collect it and fought wars for it. The stone is so
iron-hard that Maoris would have to spend months or even
years working it with water and sandstone to perfect a *mere*—
a flat, pointed weapon imbued with *mana* (power) in the
process of crafting it for tribal chiefs.

Maori culture and artistic accomplishments are most visible
on the North Island and in Rotorua, supplemented by visits
to national and regional museums and meeting house sites,
including: Auckland's War Memorial Museum; regional
museums at Dargaville, Matakohe, Russell and Kaitaia in the
Northland; the Taranaki Museum in New Plymouth; Hawke's
Bay Museum and Art Gallery; North Island Regional
Museum in Wanganui; Wellington's National Museum and
Art Gallery; Christchurch's Canterbury Museum; and
Dunedin's Otago Museum.

ITINERARY

TOUR 1 Arrive in Auckland in the morning, get settled into your accommodation, then relax and enjoy a leisurely visit to Queen Street, the spine of the city centre, with side streets climbing the hillsides. Have a snack lunch at the waterfront, then vist the Auckland Visitors' Bureau, the NZ Government Tourist Bureau or AA New Zealand for information, brochures, maps, and reservations as needed for North and South Island accommodation. After dinner, call it a day early to beat jet lag.

TOUR 2 Central Auckland's attractions can be seen in a full morning. Start with views of the city from either One Tree Hill or Mt. Eden. If you feel energetic and the weather is pleasant, walk along portions of the Coast-to-Coast Walkway from Waitemata Harbour to Manukau Harbour. Highlights include Albert Park, Auckland Domain and the War Memorial Museum and Wintergardens. Visit the Parnell District for lunch, followed by a walking tour among its Edwardian and Victorian houses renovated as boutiques. Afterwards head down to the harbour for a cruise in the Hauraki Gulf Maritime Park. After returning to Auckland's harbour, briefly visit the Old Auckland Customhouse before taking a 20-minute trip on the Devonport Ferry to the North Shore for sunset views from North Head or Mt. Victoria, followed by dinner in Devonport. Return to Auckland on the ferry.

TOUR 3 Take the Waitakere Range Scenic Drive, west of Auckland, to Piha's black-sand beach along the Tasman Sea. For lunch and winetasting, visit Henderson Valley vineyards in the western suburbs. Then drive east to the North Shore's beaches and bays *en route* to the Waiwera hot mineral pools, 30 miles north of Auckland. After a relaxing dip, go back to your hotel to get ready for a special dinner in Ponsonby Road.

TOUR 4 Leave early for the Bay of Islands and make scenic side trips on the way north. Following Highway 1, turn off to the east for Sandspit where the ferry departs for the beautiful, historic Kawau Island. Returning to Highway 1, make two more scenic detours: one to Mangawhai Heads and the other through Whangarei to Whangarei Heads. Then continue north along the Tutukaka Coast, which loops back to the main road. Make for the car ferry to Russell at Opua. If all

goes according to plan, you'll arrive in Russell in time to
stretch your legs climbing to the summit of Maki Hill for a
panoramic view of the town and its surroundings at sunset
before indulging in a delicious local seafood dinner. In the
evening, enjoy a few hours at the Duke of Marlborough pub,
relaxing and listening to big game fishing conversation. Stay
overnight in Russell.

TOUR 5 After a leisurely breakfast in Russell, take an all-
morning Cream Trip cruise to the outer limits of the Bay of
Islands, including a picnic lunch at Otehei Bay on
Urupukapuka Island. In the afternoon, head for Kerikeri via
Paihia, historic Waitangi and the beautiful Haruru Falls. Do
some sightseeing along Kerikeri Inlet's beautiful shoreline,
bays and coves before dinner at the Stone Store Restaurant.
Stay overnight in Kerikeri.

TOUR 6 This will be a long day of driving and sightseeing.
Check out early and head to the west coast to see the Waipoua
Kauri Sanctuary's huge and ancient kauri trees. Further
south, on the way back to Auckland, stop at Dargaville's
Northern Wairoa Museum and the outstanding Otamatea
Kauri and Pioneer Museum in Matakohe. Instead of driving
to Rotorua via Hamilton, which is the fastest and most direct
route from Auckland, drive 75 miles southeast of Auckland to
Thames on the Coromandel Peninsula. Check in and enjoy a
late but leisurely dinner overlooking the Firth of Thames.

TOUR 7 From Thames, head north along the rugged coast
for breakfast in Coromandel overlooking the harbour.
Afterwards you have a choice of going east on the unsurfaced
Highway 309 through stunning mountain scenery across the
peninsula, or north to view the breathtaking coastal scenery
from Colville to Fletcher Bay. Further north, around the
peninsula past the lovely Port Charles Harbour, you can enjoy
the beautiful white sands or Whangapou, and the pink sands
of New Chums Beach, Hahei and Hot Water Beach. Stop to
dig your own thermal hot pools and have a picnic lunch. After
lunch move on to Whitianga, renowned for big game fishing,
diving and underwater photography, and then to the even
more spectacular coastline from Mercury Bay to Waihi Beach.
From Waihi Beach, follow the Bay of Plenty through
Tauranga and Mount Maunganui. Then turn inland from the
Bay of Plenty's beaches to Rotorua.

TOUR 8 In Rotorua you're in the midst of an amazing

thermal region. Explore an incredible assortment of geysers, hot springs, steaming cliffs and boiling mud pools. Visit trout pools in beautiful forest parks fed by enormous quantities of spring water. Learn about Maori culture, arts and crafts in New Zealand's largest concentration of Maoris and their national cultural centre. After experiencing these thermal wonders (possibly including a flightseeing trip that lands on Mount Tarawera's summit), enjoy the unique experience of a Maori *hangi* feast and entertainment in Rotorua.

TOUR 9 Leave early in the morning for a drive to Aratiatia Rapids and Huka Falls on the Waikato River and a visit to the geothermal power project to the south, all on the way to Taupo. After lunch in Taupo, drive to Turangi to spend a while trout fishing in the Tongariro River and its tributaries, or to watch trout from behind glass in a trout hatchery. Then drive along Tongariro National Park to Ohakune, the centre of park activities, and up the slopes of Mt. Ruapehu. Afterwards continue driving to Wanganui to visit one of the most picturesque cities in New Zealand, aptly called the 'Garden City'.

TOUR 10 The parks and gardens of Wanganui are a perfect place to wind down and relax. Visit the Wanganui Museum, one of the country's best regional museums. Then have a picnic lunch in the beautiful Virginia Lake Park. After lunch take a paddlesteamer trip to Holly Lodge East Winery and from there a jetboat ride to Hipango Park. After returning to Wanganui, drive south past a string of scenic beach settlements along the Tasman Sea to New Zealand's capital, Wellington.

TOUR 11 Set in a green amphitheatre on a sparkling harbour, Wellington is at its best viewed from the heights of Mt. Victoria and from the 24-mile Marine Drive and Miramar Peninsula, stopping along the way for a picnic lunch. Spend the afternoon touring Wellington, including the Parliament Buildings and the National Museum. In the late afternoon, take the cable car up to Kelburn terminal for a stroll through the Botanic Gardens followed by dinner overlooking the city and harbour.

TOUR 12 Sail early on the Inter-Island Ferry (with breakfast on board) across Cook Strait from Wellington to Picton at the head of Queen Charlotte Sound in Marlborough Sounds. Trains and buses await those without cars. The trip to

Christchurch takes five to six hours. Dinner in this English city setting is followed by a stroll along the beautiful Avon River to parks, gardens and other urban attractions within a short distance of the tree-shaded riverbanks.

TOUR 13 Tour the inner city and outskirts of Christchurch. Visit the Botanic Gardens, Hadley Park and Cathedral Square. Perhaps hire a canoe and follow the Avon for a tour of local architecture, stopping for a riverside picnic lunch. In the afternoon, take a round trip on the scenic North and South Summit Road to Lyttelton Harbour. Pass through Port Hills for wonderful sunset views while strolling on bush walkways. Return to your hotel to get ready for dinner and an evening of entertainment at the Christchurch Arts Centre.

TOUR 14 This morning travel south across sheep-covered plains from Christchurch through Fairlie and Burke's Pass, past the blue-green and turquoise glacial Lakes Tekapo and Pukaki to Mt. Cook National Park. Walkers, climbers, rafters and skiers will find a feast of activities. After lunch, if at all possible, take a ski-plane flightseeing trip to the Tasman Glacier. Upon returning, drive through the tussock-covered expanses of the Mackenzie Basin, with a brief stop at Lake Ohau. Follow the Southern Alps over Lindis Pass to Queenstown, gateway to the wonders of Fiordland.

TOUR 15 Few places in the world have more variety of year-round lake, mountain and river recreational attractions than Queenstown and vicinity. After breakfast and booking excursions in the town centre, start the day with a leisurely cruise on the beautiful Lake Wakatipu on the coal-burning *S.S. Earnslaw.* A trip to Queenstown would not be complete without a jetboat or white-water rafting trip on one of Otago's gold-bearing rivers. After lunch in Arrowtown, a pretty relic of the gold mining era, take a pony trek to Moke Lake or spend an exciting afternoon travelling by four-wheel drive vehicle up Skippers Canyon above the Shotover River. In the evening, a gondola ride from the town centre up to Bob's Peak for dinner and spectacular views of the lake, mountains and Queenstown completes a perfect day.

TOUR 16 With an early start from Queenstown, head for Te Anau and Lake Manapouri. The first stop in Te Anau is the Fiordland National Park Headquarters. After a picnic lunch in one of Lake Te Anau's most picturesque inlets, visit Te Anau Caves' glowworm caves, or take a launch tour of the West

Arm followed by a bus or floatplane trip to Doubtful Sound
for a two-hour cruise. In the evening have a relaxing dinner in
Te Anau.

TOUR 17 Rudyard Kipling aptly described Milford Sound as
'the eighth wonder of the world'. It is three memorable hours
from Te Anau to Milford through Eglinton and Hollyford
Valleys and the Homer Tunnel, culminating in a magnificent
one- to two-hour Milford Sound launch cruise with views of
Mitre Peak and Stirling Falls. Drive your own car and, on the
way back, you can spend extra time at several lakes and take a
short walk on one of the tracks (Hollyford, Greenstone or
Routebourne). Finish the day with dinner in Te Anau or have
a camper's meal along one of the tracks.

TOUR 18 Backtrack to Queenstown and, in good weather,
drive up the unsurfaced road to the top of the Crown Range,
then through Cardrona Valley in time for lunch in Wanaka.
Climb up Mt. Iron for the view. There's still time for superb
trout or salmon fishing in Lakes Wanaka or Hawea, kayaking
on the Motatapu River, pony-trekking or, in winter, afternoon
skiing on Cardrona. The Wanaka waterfront and nearby
Glendhu Bay are great places for after-dinner sunset strolls.

TOUR 19 Leave Wanaka very early for a full day's drive
down Makarora Valley, over Haast Pass and then to the
National Park Centre at Fox Glacier in South Westland. Plan
on making the not-too-strenuous climb to Fox Chalet
Lookout for inspiring views of Fox Glacier and the Tasman
Sea at sunset. Move on to Franz Josef Glacier for dinner and
the night.

TOUR 20 Have a hearty breakfast and leave by minibus for
the 2½ hour Franz Josef Glacier Valley Walk. Later, on the
way up the narrow Westland coastal strip to Hokitika, visit
Lake Matheson, Lake Kaniere Reserve or some of the other
beautiful small lakes *en route*. Spend the afternoon in the
Hokitika area visiting relics of the gold mining era, factories
cutting greenstone (the Maori sacred gemstone), and several
superb viewpoints, before driving to Greymouth for the night.

TOUR 21 Visit Shantytown's reconstruction of an 1860s gold
mining town near Greymouth. Then drive on to Highway 73,
Arthur's Pass Road, the most spectacular of the South
Island's alpine crossings, passing through Arthur's Pass
National Park. Plan for a lunch stop near Arthur's Pass

Village, scenic walks on several inspiring trails, and perhaps a last trout fishing excursion at Pearson Lake. Descend to Christchurch to check in and prepare for dinner in Christchurch.

TOUR 22 In the morning head for Banks Peninsula, with beautiful coastal stretches dotted with sleepy towns. Enjoy lunch and sightseeing in Akaroa, the charming Victorian village with an historic touch of French in its architecture and signs. On the way back to Christchurch in the afternoon, stop at Okains Bay and several other villages on the Peninsula. Celebrate the conclusion of the trip this evening with a de-luxe dinner in Christchurch.

TOUR 1

ARRIVE IN AUCKLAND

Welcome to New Zealand! Ease into the comfortable Kiwi
lifestyle and pace. Spend the day in Auckland, settling into
your hotel and getting acquainted with the central city,
Parnell and the harbour. While you're in Queen Street, stop
at the New Zealand Tourist and Publicity travel office
(NZTP) to book future accommodation, transport, sightseeing
and other tours in the Auckland region and elsewhere in New
Zealand, and gather information and maps for the rest of your
trip.

Suggested schedule

Arrive at Auckland International Airport.

Take a bus or taxi to town or directly to your
accommodation and check in.
Enjoy a relaxing breakfast or lunch in Parnell
before exploring the city.
Book future accommodation, transport and
excursions at the NZTP office.
Ease into Auckland's nightlife with the
expectation of an early start the next morning.

Auckland orientation

Auckland straddles a narrow isthmus between two harbours:
Manukau on the west and Waitemata on the east merging into
Hauraki Gulf. The Harbour Bridge across Waitemata
Harbour links the city with the rapidly growing North Shore.
Over a quarter of New Zealand's population (850,000) lives in
Auckland, mostly in bungalows, an urbanised network of
villages sprawling over a hilly region of volcanoes. A large
Maori community and immigrants from Europe, Asia and the
Pacific Islands give Auckland a cosmopolitan flavour. With
over 70,000 Polynesians, Auckland is the world's largest
Polynesian centre. Niueans and Cook Islanders, Samoans and
Tongans add interest and vitality to city life.

See the city tomorrow from several vantage points: the twin
cones of Mt. Victoria and North Head across the Waitemata
Harbour; One Tree Hill and Mt. Eden, part of a
Coast-to-Coast Walkway from Waitemata Harbour to

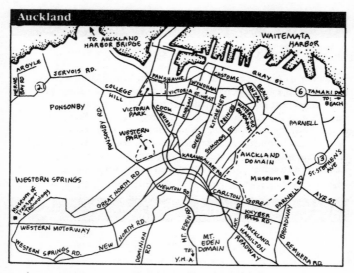

Manukau Harbour; and the Waitakere Scenic Drive west of
the city. Discover Auckland's beautiful parks, especially
Victorian Albert Park in the city centre and Cornwall Park,
with sheep and cattle grazing on its slopes, which merges with
One Tree Hill.

Lower Queen Street is Auckland's main street. From the
Ferry Terminal on the wide and busy Quay Street, Queen
Street is filled with shops, arcades and offices. The street has
little charm but plenty of choices. From the Ferry Terminal,
catch the ferry to Devonport on the North Shore or, from
nearby wharves, launch trips to Hauraki Gulf Islands. Queen
Elizabeth Square at the bottom of Queen Street contains the
central post office, shopping complex (more shops and the
city's duty-free shop) and offices.

Browse in craft shops, antique shops, art galleries and
boutiques in the surbubs of Parnell along Parnell Road,
with its renovated Victorian and Edwardian buildings, as
well as in Remuera, Ponsonby, Victoria Park Market's
food and craft market, and the colourful Karangahape
Road, opposite Grafton Bridge, where many Pacific Islanders
shop.

If you arrive on Saturday, central Auckland is best seen
before noon, when many shops, cafes and restaurants close. If
you arrive on Sunday, take the day off like everyone else.
Depending on the weather, join the droves heading for

beaches and the sea. Otherwise, get lost in the fabulous War
Memorial Museum.

From airport to accommodation

Auckland International Airport lies 13 miles south of the city.
The terminal contains a Travellers' Information Centre (tel.
275-7467) open Monday to Sunday, 6:30 a.m. to 11:00 p.m.,
bank, post office, hire car desk and even a shower.

Between 6:00 a.m. and 9:00 p.m., coaches leave regularly
for the City Airline Terminal at the corner of Quay and
Albert Streets. The fare is NZ$4 (£1.60). On request, the
driver will drop you off at city hotels on the direct bus route.
Taxi fares to the city centre are about NZ$25 (£10) on
weekdays and slightly higher at weekends. Touristop Tourist
Services Ltd. in the City Airline Terminal is open all week
from 8:30 a.m. to 4:30 p.m. (tel. 775-783). Arriving in
Auckland at the weekend without a room reservation can be a
problem. The Travellers' Information Centre at the airport
will book accommodation or, after arriving in central
Auckland, turn immediately to the New Zealand Government
Tourist Bureau (NZGTB), 99 Queen Street (tel. 798-180), for
booking assistance (8:30 a.m. to 5:00 p.m. weekdays and 9:30
a.m. to noon on Saturdays). NZGTB has a NZ$2 (£0.80)
booking fee. The Automobile Association, 33 Wyndham
Street (tel. 774-660), can be just as helpful if you bring your
AA membership card. The Auckland Youth Hostel (YH)
office, open from 8:30 a.m. to 4:30 p.m., is in Australia
House, 36 Customs Street East (794-224), very close to the
Bus Terminal and the Percy Shieff Hostel (794-258). The
Best Western/New Zealand Reservation Service (tel. 792-854)
provides a 24-hour booking service and has numerous
properties in the Auckland area with NZ$40–$50 (£16–£20)
rates.

In addition to the NZGTB, the Auckland Visitors' Bureau,
299 Queen Street at Aotea Square, has all the maps,
information and guidebooks you could possibly need for the
next few days, including brochures on Auckland's latticework
of signposted walkways, parks, reserves, botanic gardens and
dozens of gulf islands.

City transport

A car is convenient but not essential to see Auckland. You
don't have to hire a car until Tour 3. Buses of the Auckland
Regional Authority (ARA) and suburban companies run
frequently to most central and outlying areas from the Central
Bus Centre (tel. 797-119 between 6:00 a.m. and 11:00 p.m.

for information) in Commerce Street behind the main post
office. In addition to the main ARA terminal, there are four
suburban centres: in New Lynn, Onehunga, Panmure, and
Otahuhu. Timetables and tickets can be obtained from kiosks
at these places or The Bus Place (131 Hobson Street, Mon.-
Fri., 8:15 a.m. to 4:30 p.m.). Phone Buz-a-Bus (tel. 797-119)
between 6:00 a.m. and 11:00 p.m. weekdays), tell them where
you want to go and they'll provide timetable information.

Ask about 10-journey tickets and family passes for about
NZ$5 (£2). A Busabout Day Pass, which can be bought from
a bus driver, costs NZ$4.30 (£1.70) adult, NZ$2 (£0.80) child
(or, for two days, NZ$7 (£2.80) adult, NZ$3.60 (£1.40) child)
for unlimited ARA bus travel after 9:00 a.m. on weekdays and
any time at weekends and holidays.

For cycle touring, call at the Visitors Bureau and pick up a
bicycle route map covering about 30 miles around Auckland.
Most cycle shops around town hire bicycles. At weekends
cycle hire is available at The Domain, along the waterfront
and in Devonport on the North Shore.

Where to shop

Parnell's upmarket shopping in one of Auckland's oldest
districts benefits from imaginative restoration creating
boutiques for fashions, pottery, glassware, jewellery, antiques
and various craft items, along with a variety of good quality
restaurants and pleasant shops for snacks and refreshments. In
and near Parnell Road are historic church buildings, like St.
Stephen's and St. Mary's, and some fine old 19th century
buildings open to the public. From November to March, see
the lovely rose gardens in nearby Sir Dove-Meyer Robinson
Park.

Ponsonby's exclusive boutiques stand side-by-side with
shops catering to the day-to-day needs of local Polynesians. In
Karangahape Road (called 'K Road' by local residents) many
shops are stocked with Polynesian foods. On Sunday at noon
there's a popular market at the corner of K Road and
Ponsonby Road. While in the Ponsonby District for shopping
or dining, visit Renall Street with about 20 preserved 19th
century cottages, privately owned and not open to the public
but worth seeing from the outside.

Visit the Otara Shopping Centre car park on Sunday
morning for more Polynesian shopping activity.

Cook Street and Victoria Park are busy and entertaining
bazaar-style markets. The Cook Street Market is in Aotea
Square on Friday from 9:00 a.m. to 8:00 p.m., Saturday from
10:00 a.m. to 4:00 p.m. and Sunday from 10:00 a.m. to 3:00

p.m. Victoria Park Market, Victoria Street West, from 9:00 a.m. to 7:00 p.m. seven days a week, gathers weavers, potters, leather-workers and other crafts people in the midst of a fruit and vegetable market.

Where to stay

Start experiencing New Zealand hospitality at a B&B in Auckland. I like staying near Parnell, with its nearby restaurants and cafes and a number of good and inexpensive lodgings. The best B&B bargain is the charming **Ascot Parnell**, 36 St. Stephens Avenue, Parnell, Auckland, tel. 399-012, a completely restored and well-maintained house dating back to 1910, with spacious, elegant rooms, some with private baths, and complete breakfasts, for NZ$20 (£8) single or NZ$39 (£16) double. It's well worth booking far in advance.

Another excellent way to start your stay in Auckland is to head from the airport to the cheerful rooms and stained-glass windows of **Heathmaur Lodge**, tel. 763-527, at 75 Argyle Street overlooking Herne Bay. Make reservations in advance for the first night. Otherwise, like many of Auckland's B&Bs, it may be full.

The **Grande Vue**, 3 Princes Street, tel. 793-965, opposite the Inter-Continental Hotel, is one of the best central budget B&Bs, at about NZ$26 (£10) for a single. If all of its 19 rooms are booked, try the nearby **Arundel Tourist Hotel**, 12 Waterloo Quadrant, tel. 734-828, no longer the best value for budgeteers but full of character and charm, priced at NZ$30 (£12) for a B&B single. Single travellers may have a better chance at the **Rosanna Travel Hotel**, 217 Ponsonby Road, tel. 766-603, with its five single rooms, NZ$20 (£8) with breakfast and without a private bath. Budget travellers with large appetites will love the **Aspen Lodge Bed and Breakfast Tourist Hotel** at 62 Emily Place, tel. 796-698, from NZ$29 (£12) with all-you-can-eat continental breakfasts. **Mt. Eden Youth Hostel**, 5A Oaklands Road, Mount Eden, tel. 603-975, housing 46 people for NZ$9.50 (£4) each per night, is about three miles south of the city centre. Take bus number 273, 274 or 275 from the central bus station. The **Percy Shieff Youth Hostel**, 7 Princes Street, Auckland, tel. 700-258, for NZ$9.50 (£4) per night, has 74 beds in 11 rooms. Located across the street from the Hyatt, it is within walking distance of everything. The **YMCA**, corner of Pitt Street and Grays Avenue, Auckland, tel. 32-068, has singles for men and women, dinner and breakfast, excellent value at NZ$20.50 (£8) per night. Much further from the city, at 14

Shirley Road, Western Springs, tel. 862-800, but right near
the Museum of Transport and Technology and the Zoo, with
good bus access, **Ivanhoe Travellers Lodge** offers a
dormitory bed at NZ$9.50 (£4) and perfectly adequate single
rooms for NZ$14 (£5.50). **Hekerua House**, tel. 72-8371, at
Onetangi on Waiheke Island, with private rooms and a
dormitory, is the best get-away-from-it-all budget hostel in
the region. Rates start at NZ$8 (£3).

    The James Cook Motel, 320 Parnell Road, tel. 33-460,
costs NZ$35 (£14) for two people. Budget-watchers travelling
together who want to be near Parnell Village can find five
charming rooms in a lodge in the **Barrycourt Motor Inn**
grounds, 10-20 Gladstone Road, tel. 33-789, priced at NZ$45
(£18) for one or two people. The **Casa Mia**, 481 Parnell
Road, tel. 790-436, is small, pleasant and only NZ$16 (£6.50)
per night. During university vacations, Spartan budget
travellers can try the **Norman Spencer**, 9 St. Stephens
Avenue, Parnell, tel. 799-911, for about NZ$7 (£3) single
with your own sleeping bag. The **Manor House Hotel**, 363
Queen Street, tel. 778-542, has a very convenient location and
simple, clean, adequately spacious rooms at NZ$25 (£10)
single, with a shared bath. With hearty breakfasts that make
up for smaller rooms, the **Aspen Lodge**, 62 Emily Place, tel.
796-698, compares favourably with the Manor in all other
respects, with NZ$26 (£10.50) singles. **Farthings Hotel**, 131
Beach Road, tel. 30-629, has a great variety of inexpensive
rooms for couples, groups and families of all ages; 75 rooms to
choose from starting at NZ$30 (£12) for a single without
private bath.

    Families might prefer **Campbell Court Motel**, across
from Cornwall Park, 317 Manukau Road, Epsom 3, Auckland,
tel. 686-409, for rooms with kitchens, sleeping up to six,
laundry facilities, telephones and even colour TV. Continental
and cooked breakfasts are available. Rates start at NZ$35
(£14); each additional person NZ$8 (£3); and under 12 NZ$4
(£1.60). Both city and airport buses stop right at the gate.
With more rooms, as well as sauna, swimming and spa pools,
the quiet **Mt. Eden Motel**, 47 Balmoral Road, Mt. Eden,
Auckland, tel. 687-187, has about the same rates and also a
very good bus service.

Where to eat

Auckland has an underrated collection of restaurants. Even
the city's residents are so defensive about their cuisine that
the restaurant situation seems much more bleak than it really
is. Dining in Auckland may not be one of the best reasons for

visiting New Zealand but, especially thanks to the French
influence, there are plenty of very good moderate to higher-
priced eating places to choose from.

Victoria Park Market, in Victoria Street across from
Victoria Park, has pies, hot dogs, pastas, salads and a variety
of other standard and ethnic foods for hungry budget
travellers. At **Rick's Cafe American** (tel. 399-074) in the
market you can have jacket potatoes and spare ribs served in
Bogart decor. For comparable variety and inexpensive food,
the **Plaza Arcade** at 128 Queen Street has 12 international
food shops covering from Bali to Britain. **Armadillo's**, 178
Symonds Street, tel. 393-744, has huge hamburgers, good
salads and amusing reminders of the old west. If you're a
sucker for great pie, try their pecan pie a la mode. For
Mexican food, the **Mexican Cafe**, 67 Victoria Street West,
tel. 732-311, is the only place to go. After the long climb up
Mt. Eden—or even if you drive—try a bowl of **Chez
Daniel**'s onion soup at 597 Mt. Eden Road, tel. 689-676.

For inexpensive Italian food, pizza or exotic dishes like
chicken stuffed with peanuts, make for **Collage**, right in the
heart of town at 26 Lorne Street, tel. 33-086. For even bigger
appetites for Italian food, at NZ$10 (£4) or under, it's **La
Bussola**, 17 Great North Road, Ponsonby, tel. 768-597, or
La Trattoria, 259 Parnell Road, tel. 795-58.

The ten-course buffet lunch, 12:00 noon to 2:30 p.m.
weekdays at the **New Orient Restaurant** (Strand Arcade,
tel. 797-793), is delicious and less expensive than meals in
other Chinese restaurants. Avoid disappointment with seafood
fare by going to the **Union Fish Company**'s old brick
warehouse, 16 Quay Street, tel. 796-745, replete with
maritime decor. You can fit the meal to your wallet there, but
even better seafood value is the tiny **Waterfront Cafe**, Ferry
Building, Quay Street, tel. 732-770. Another top spot for a
seafood lunch is **Sitting Duck** in Westhaven Marina (tel.
760-374) which offers top value for the combination of view,
menu and price.

Fresh mussels are well prepared and reasonably priced at
the **Front Page Cafe**, 163 Symonds Street, tel. 733-579. For
innovative seafood menus, visit **Flamingos**, 242 Jervois
Road, Herne Bay, tel. 765-899.

Ponsonby Road is the hands-down winner as the street with
the greatest number and variety of excellent restaurants—
mostly expensive. Jervois Road and Herne Bay, in Upper
Ponsonby, add to Ponsonby's culinary clout. The epicurean
safari in Ponsonby Road follows ascending street numbers.
Take your choice. How could you leave New Zealand without

at least one first-rate game dish with the right wine? **Colin Brown's Gamekeeper**, 29 Ponsonby Road, tel. 789-052 is one of the best choices. Stuffed calamari at **Franco's One on the Side**, 42A Ponsonby Road, tel. 790-471; perhaps a very formal and expensive dinner under the chandeliers at **Orsini's**, 50 Ponsonby Road, tel. 764-563; an impeccably served meal of lamb fillets wrapped in spinach followed by a banana soufflé or coffee marshmallow ice cream at **Wheelers**, 43 Ponsonby Road, tel. 763-185; a lamb dinner outside on a summer night at the **Bronze Goat**, 108 Ponsonby Road, tel. 768-193; lunch in **Oblio**'s garden conservatory, 110 Ponsonby Road, tel. 763-041; Sunday brunch and jazz at **Carthews**, 151 Ponsonby Road; a seafood dinner before an evening out at **Peppermint Park**, 161 Ponsonby Road, tel. 768-689; fish of the day immersed in the **Jungle Cafe**'s greenery, 222 Ponsonby Road, tel. 767-888; and last but not least, seafood chowder at **Fed Up**, 244 Ponsonby Road, tel. 768-469.

Believe it or not, Auckland has respectable French cuisine. Tony Astle's **Antoine's**, 333 Parnell Road, tel. 798-756, in an old restored house next to Parnell Village, serves excellent French food in very formal, traditional French colonial decor and atmosphere at an appropriately stiff price, NZ$110–$140 (£44–£56) for two with wine. The international award-winning dishes of Warwick Brown's **Le Gourmet**, 1 Williamson Avenue, Ponsonby, tel. 769-499, are worthy of any major city and, not surprisingly, expensive. Other excellent 'splashing out' restaurants include: the **French Cafe**, 210B Court, Symonds Street, tel. 771-911; **Hoffman's**, 70 Jervois Road, Herne Bay, tel. 762-049; **Delmonico's** in the Hotel de Brett, High Street, tel. 32-389, and Hyatt's **Top of the Town**, tel. 797-220.

Bagatelle, 279 Parnell Road, tel. 396-289, one of Auckland's unsung heroes of French provincial cuisine, offers much more casual and less pricey French fare than Antoine's just down the street. Or try either of these outstanding French provincial restaurants: **Anatole's**, 35 Cook Street, tel. 534-3142, in the eastern suburbs or **Le Brie**, on the corner of Chancery and Warspite Streets, tel. 733-935. Delicious fish, fowl, and fillet along with friendly service in any of these three restaurants comes to NZ$50–60 (£20–£24) for two, BYO (bring your own wine).

The search for Auckland's best fillet steak ends at **Harleys**, 25 Anzac Avenue, tel. 735-801. For stuffed venison roast and complementary ambience, visit **Le Rendezvous**, 473 Khyber Pass Road, Newmarket, tel. 540-903.

TOUR 2

AROUND AUCKLAND

A full morning in Auckland covers the best viewpoints, parks and museums, followed by lunch and a walking tour in the Parnell District. Afterwards take a 1½ hour cruise in the Hauraki Gulf. Return for a bit of sightseeing in town before taking a 20-minute ferry trip to the North Shore for sunset sightseeing and dinner. Return to Auckland by ferry in the late evening.

Suggested schedule

7:00 a.m.	Early breakfast
8:00 a.m.	Catch a bus from the Central Bus Terminal to Cornwall Park and One Tree Hill or Mt. Eden Domain for easy walking and views.
10:30 a.m.	Tour the Auckland Domain, War Memorial Museum and Wintergardens possibly on an Auckland City Council guided walk.
12:00 noon	Lunch in Parnell
1:30 p.m.	Mt. Cook Auckland Harbour cruise
4:00 p.m.	Return to town and visit the Old Auckland Customhouse
.5:00 p.m.	Ferry to Devonport for a walk and sunset sightseeing at North Head and nearby Mt. Victoria.
6:30 p.m.	Dinner in Devonport at Rickerby's or Rocks Restaurant.
8:30 p.m.	Return to city by ferry.

Transport

The Ferry Building Information Centre has all the harbour information and timetables. The Devonport Ferry Service departs seven days a week from the Queens Wharf, the terminal behind the Ferry Building in Quay Street, crossing the harbour in 20 minutes to Devonport on the North Shore, for NZ$3.25 (£1.30) adult, NZ$1.65 (£0.67) child (round trip). The ferry leaves Queens Wharf every hour on the hour, and leaves Devonport Wharf on the half-hour (until 11:30 p.m., Monday to Saturday). Captain Cook Cruises Ltd. (tel. 774-074), in Quay Street, offers a variety of cruises around

the harbour: morning tea cruises, 9:45 to 11:30 a.m. (NZ$18
(£7)); volcanic island cruise, 9:45 a.m. to 2:30 p.m. (NZ$38
(£15)); lunch cruise, noon to 2:15 p.m. (NZ$28 (£11));
afternoon tea cruise, 2:30 p.m. to 4:00 p.m. (NZ$18 (£7)); an
evening cruise, Monday to Thursday, 6:45 to 9:15 p.m.
(NZ$24 (£9.50)); and a sunset cocktail cruise, Friday,
Saturday and Sunday, 6:00 to 8:00 p.m. (NZ$22 (£9)). Blue
Boats (tel. 34-479) runs a ferry service between the North
Shore (Launch Steps next to Prince Wharf) and the city and
also conducts a one-hour harbour cruise for only NZ$5 (£2).

Sightseeing highlights

●●●**The Domain** is a beautiful park setting for the War
Memorial Museum, Wintergardens, Fern Glen, Planetarium
and Herb Garden. The Auckland City Council's (tel. 792-020)
free two-hour guided walk around the central city, featuring
The Domain, is an excellent introduction to the city.

●●●**The War Memorial Museum** on a grassy hilltop in
Auckland Domain, has outstanding views of Waitemata
Harbour and the North Shore. Even if you're not fond of
museums, don't miss its outstanding display of Maori and
Pacific Island artefacts, natural history exhibits covering the
gamut of New Zealand's flora and fauna, sea life, geology and
palaeontology, maritime history exhibits, and a planetarium
(Saturday and Sunday shows). The Museum's 'Centennial
Street' is a reconstruction of an Auckland shopping street of
1866. September to May, open 10:00 a.m. to 5:00 p.m. (4:15
p.m. in winter), Monday to Saturday, and Sunday 11:00 a.m.
to 5:00 p.m.; June to August, 10:00 a.m. to 4:15 p.m.
Admission free.

●●**Wintergardens** in the museum grounds in the Domain
holds over 10,000 South Pacific plants in a Cool House, and
an amazing variety of hothouse plants in the Tropical House
and the Fernery. Open 10:00 a.m. to 4:00 p.m.

●●●**Mount Eden**, Auckland's highest point (643 feet),
offers the finest views over the city, surrounding water and
the Waitakere Ranges. Walk or drive up Mountain Road to
the summit. This volcano crater was used as an ancient Maori
fortress, and defence terraces and storage pits can still be seen
around the sides. Mount Eden is part of the Coast-to-Coast
Walkway. It is closer to the centre than One Tree Hill. Seeing
both Mt. Eden and One Tree Hill requires a very early start.
Catch a bus from the Central Bus Terminal to either vantage
point.

●●**One Tree Hill and Cornwall Park**—The terraced
volcanic cone rises above Cornwall Park, which includes

Acacia Cottage, Auckland's oldest wooden building (1841).
Walk or drive past sheep-filled fields to the summit of what
was once the home of the region's largest Maori settlement.
● **The Old Auckland Customhouse**, at the corner of
Custom and Albert Streets near the harbour, has been
renovated in French Rennaisance style into a shopping
emporium with a restaurant, bar and cinema. See the central
Auckland branch of the Clevedon Woolshed, with its great
selection of knitwear, weaving, sheepskins, accessories and
gifts.
● ● **The Devonport Ferry** to the North Shore is one of the
best ways to see Auckland from the water. The ferry service
includes the *Kestrel*, built in 1905 and beautifully refurbished.
Walk up to North Head for a good viewing point or up
nearby Mt. Victoria (250 feet) for panoramic views. The
ferries run until 11:00 p.m., Monday to Saturday, until 9:45
on Sunday.

Where to eat
Take an evening ferry trip to Devonport for a stuffed leg of
rabbit dinner and scrumptious desserts at **Rickerby's**, Fleet
Street, Devonport, tel. 457-072. For reasonable seafood dishes
with great harbour views in Devonport, try **Rocks**, 33 King
Edward Parade, tel. 451-455. Also on the North Shore, **J.C.'s**,
Beach Road, Rothesay Bay, tel. 478-8123, has superb dishes,
decor and service. All three restaurants offer a great way to
end a day of exploring nearby beaches and the harbour.

Itinerary options
The **Coast-to-Coast Walkway** is marked by signs between
the Waitemata Harbour on the east coast and the Manukau
Harbour on the west. The Walkway connects Albert Park,
Auckland University, Auckland Domain, Mt. Eden, One Tree
Hill, and other points of interest, keeping to reserves wherever
possible. At an easy pace, the eight-mile walk can be done in
four hours, near bus routes all the way.
    For those who want a more leisurely walk, the Auckland
City Council offers a series of free guided walks that take
about 1½ hours each. **Albert Park** with its woods, daffodils,
tropical glass house, cricket grounds and the remains of Albert
Barracks, built in the 1840s against Maori attacks, is located
in the Auckland University grounds behind the main library.
The **City Art Gallery**, in a French Renaissance-style
building at the south-west corner of Albert Park, houses the
country's most complete collection of New Zealand art,
starting with early European settlement, as well as

international and contemporary art. Open from 10:00 a.m. to 4:30 p.m. on weekdays (6:30 p.m. on Friday) and 1:00 to 5:30 p.m. on Saturday and Sunday. Admission free.

The **Museum of Transport and Technology**, commonly referred to as MOTAT, in Great North Road in the Western Springs District contains an interesting collection of everything that buzzes, spins, calculates and moves, from musical boxes and vintage motor cars to steam locomotives. A whole building of early flying machines features the remarkable inventions of Richard Pearse, whose aircraft first flew in 1902—shades of the Wright Brothers. The site's old buildings have been restored as a pioneer village. An electric tram runs regularly between MOTAT and the Auckland Zoo. Open daily from 9:00 a.m. to 5:00 p.m., weekends 10:00 a.m. to 5:00 p.m. Admission NZ$6 (£2.40) adult, NZ$3 (£1.20) child.

For insatiable flying buffs, the nearby **Keith Park Memorial Airfield** houses a large collection of yesteryear's aircraft.

● ● Auckland Zoological Park, next to MOTAT, offers a chance to see kiwi birds in a special nocturnal house and the tuatara (the only remaining link with the dinosaur), in addition to a selection of over 1,500 mammals, birds, reptiles and fish. The zoo is mostly outdoors in spacious enclosures set in 45 acres of park-like gardens, with a children's zoo. Open daily from 9:30 a.m. to 5:30 p.m., last admission 4:15 p.m. Admission, NZ$6 (£2.40) adult, NZ$3 (£1.20) child.

Hauraki Gulf touring

A one-hour ferry trip (NZ$11 (£4.40) adult, NZ$5.50 (£2.20) child) to Waiheke Island, Hauraki Gulf's largest and most central island, from Half Moon Bay offers sample views of this maritime playground by day and dusk. Flying (10 minutes, NZ$42 (£17) per person return) from Ardmore and Mechanics Bay 'saves' over 1½ hours, substituting flightseeing for the experience of a leisurely Gulf boat trip. Waiheke's towns and beautiful white sand beaches are an easy walk apart, so there really is no need for a car. The Royal Forest and Bird Society's reserve at Onetangi, a bus journey from the wharf, contains over two miles of bush walks. The **Charter Cruise Company**, tel. 734-557, sails a 60-foot catamaran around the harbour and inner gulf coast for two hours. Join in the sailing activity or just watch the scenery. Adults NZ$25 (£10), children NZ$8.50 (£3.40), with a lunch option for an additional NZ$8.50 (£3.40). The **Volcanic Island Cruise,** tel. 774-074, departs daily at 9:45 a.m. and 12

noon from Launchman's Steps for Rangitoto Island, NZ$44
(£17.50) adult and NZ$24 (£9.50) child, including a bus trip
to the island's summit. **Blue Boats,** tel. 34-479, serve
Rangitoto Island, Motutapu, Motuihe, and Rakino. The daily
service departs from Launchman's Steps Monday to Friday at
9:30 a.m., on Wednesday at 7:30 a.m. and 4:30 p.m., on
Fridays at 6:00 p.m., and at weekends at 9:30 a.m. and 12:30
p.m. The ferries return Monday to Sunday at 3:00 p.m., on
Wednesday at 10:30 a.m. and 6:15 p.m., and at weekends at
5:45 p.m. Return fare, NZ$8.50 (£3.40) adults, NZ$4.20
(£1.70) children. For solitude and lonely beaches, bush walks
and a free campsite, your only access to Great Barrier Island,
55 miles out, is by amphibian (**Sea Bee Air** for NZ$132
(£53) return) or small plane. Several other airlines fly to the
islands and offer flightseeing excursions.

Region surrounding Auckland

Kiwi recreational life in Auckland revolves around water
sports. They're either in or on the water. Most people seem to
have boats or easy access to them. Little wonder with over
100 beaches within an hour's drive, dozens of offshore islands
and their hundreds of sandy coves, 57 degrees the midwinter
average temperature and eight months of the year averaging in
the high 60s and low 70s.
   On the suburban shore north of Takapuna, there is a chain
of lovely beaches that runs from Castor Bay northward to
Long Bay. The Wenderholm and Mahurangi Heads are
special reserves with natural beauty and uncrowded shores.
Starting at the city's waterfront, the seven-mile scenic Tamaki
Drive follows the south shore of Waitemata Harbour to St.
Heliers Bay. Tamaki Drive, from Mission Beach, only 15
minutes from the waterfront, is a scenic road and bicycle
route that passes through a series of beachfront suburban
'villages', each with its own quiet character. Combine a trip
down Tamaki Drive with a visit to either the **Bay
Restaurant,** in Mission Bay, tel. 581-879, or **Lizzie's,** tel.
583-930, just down the street. Both have surprisingly
sophisticated fare for a little eastern hamlet, such as superb
seafood and salmon mousse, and charge accordingly. Both
offer nice views of the Bay and Rangitoto Island and pleasant
decor.

TOUR 3

WAITAKERE RANGE AND NORTH SHORE

Spend the morning exploring the tracks and vistas of the Waitakere Range and the black-sand beach at Piha along the Tasman Sea. Then drive to the Henderson Valley's vineyards for lunch and wine-tasting. In the afternoon follow the North Shore's lovely beaches and bays to a dip in the Waiwera hot springs before a farewell-to-Auckland dinner at one of Ponsonby Road's many restaurants.

Suggested schedule

7:30 a.m.	After breakfast hire a car.
9:00 a.m.	Waitakere Range Scenic Drive.
11:00 a.m.	Piha or other black-sand beaches.
1:00 p.m.	Henderson Valley vineyards for lunch.
3:00 p.m.	Sightsee along North Shore beaches and bays.
4:30 p.m.	Enjoy Waiwera natural hot springs.
7:00 p.m.	Clean up and change for dinner.
8:30 p.m.	Dinner.

Driving to the Waitakere Range and Henderson Valley

Most major car hire companies operate in Auckland:

Avis—22 Wakefield Street, tel. 792-545.

Budget—26 Nelson Street, tel. 734-949.

Hertz—154 Victoria Street W., tel. 34-924.

Cars are expensive unless you have a discount voucher purchased as part of a package at home. Beware of cut rates and special deals for cars that may turn out to be problems. If you hire a car, arrange to drop it off in Wellington without a penalty charge.

From the central area, take Symonds Street over the Route 1 Motorway to Dominion Road (Route 4) south-west to Hillsborough Road (Route 15, which changes its name several times), then westward to Titirangi Road (Route 24) which becomes the Waitakere Scenic Drive. The Information Centre is about three miles from the intersection of Routes 15 and 24 on your left. About three miles past the Information Centre is the turnoff (Piha Road) to Piha Beach. As you drive down

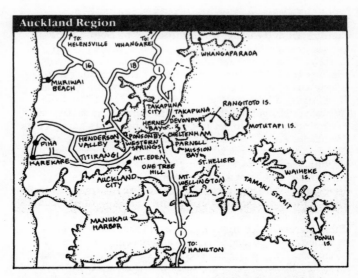

this secondary road, you'll see tracks heading into the bush to your right (north). This winding road covers about nine miles and takes half an hour to Piha Beach.

From the intersection of Piha Road and Scenic Drive, continue north along Scenic Drive for about another six miles to the intersection with Mountain Road on your right. Mountain Road will take you into Henderson Valley to the vineyards.

Driving from Henderson Valley to the North Shore, take Henderson Valley Road to Henderson. Turn right along Great North Road (Route 16) and then left along Te Atatu to Motorway 16 east through the centre to Motorway 1, which crosses Waitemata Harbour to the North Shore. Leave it at Takapuna-Devonport in Esmond Road (Route 26), turning left along the coastal road which heads north past the East Coast Bays (Milford, Castor Bay, Campbells Bay and others). At Long Bay, turn west briefly to the Old East Coast Road, which merges with Motorway 1 North just before Silverdale. Take Motorway 1 to Waiwera. Return to Auckland later on Motorway 1.

Sightseeing highlights
● ● ●**Waitakere Range Scenic Drive** within the Centennial Memorial Regional Park offers several spectacular views of Buckland and the Gulf, especially Pakinson's Lookout, Pukematekeo Lookout and View Road up to the

summit of Mt. Atkinson. The Scenic Drive, a tarred road
running from Titirangi to Swanson via the Summit Ridge,
passes through fine forests, with views over the city and
harbour. Stands of huge ancient kauri trees remain along the
walking tracks that thread through the thick bush. Fine
specimens of kauri trees and regeneration can be found at
Titirangi and Piha Valley. The forest-covered hills of the
Waitakere Ranges are threaded with walking tracks through
bush thick enough to get lost in. ARA publishes a map of the
Waitakere Ranges covering 135 walking tracks in the area.
Public buses do not run to the Waitakere. For those not
driving, catch a bus to Titirangi and be prepared to walk or
hitch-hike. The Arataki Information Centre, tel.
Turangi/TGN 7134, is on the Scenic Drive a couple of miles
from Titirangi. It doesn't open until 1:00 p.m. on weekdays,
10:00 a.m. on weekends. The black-sand beaches of Muriwau,
Piha, Karekare and the Tasman west coast are wild and
treacherous favourites of surfers and daring swimmers. The
Waitakere Ranges rise between the city and these west coast
beaches. These beaches are accessible from trails winding
down to the sand from the rim of mountains. Only swim in
the rough surf near life-savers patrolling the beaches.

● ●**Henderson Valley's vineyards,** on the lower slopes of
the Waitakere Range in the western suburbs, produce some
first-rate wines that can be tasted in pleasant outdoor
restaurants. Almost a dozen wineries were established by
Dalmatian settlers who came from Yugoslavia in the early
1900s to work in Northland's kauri gum fields.

● ●**North Shore beaches and bays** stretch from Takapuna
and Castor Bay to Long Bay, with East Coast Bays Cliff
Walks providing wonderful views of the Hauraki Gulf islands.

●**The Waiwera Hot Pools Leisure Resort,** tel. 42-65-369,
about 30 miles north of Auckland adjoining the Waiwera
Hotel, has public and private hot mineral pools, with varying
temperatures, private saunas, suntan beds and sun lounges,
and water slides for children. Open every day until late
evening. Within walking distance of Waiwera, Wenderholm
Regional Park offers an excellent combination day-trip of
bush walking, hot pools and ocean swimming.

TOUR 4

AUCKLAND TO THE BAY OF ISLANDS

The drive from Auckland to Russell in the Bay of Islands includes side-trips to Kawau Island and scenic coastal areas south and north of Whangarei. Take the Opua car ferry to Russell. The day ends in Russell—known as the hellhole of the Pacific in the early 1800s, first capital of New Zealand. Today, historic Russell is an ideal touring base for the Bay of Islands Maritime and Historic Park and its 150 islands.

Suggested schedule

7:00 a.m.	Breakfast, check out and departure from Auckland.
10:30 a.m.	Ferry from Sandspit to Kawau Island.
2:30 p.m.	Return to Sandspit and continue north to Mangawhai Heads and Tutukaka Coast.
5:30 p.m.	Opua car ferry to Russell.
6:00 p.m.	Arrive in Russell. Check in and head for the public bar at the Duke of Marlborough Hotel for refreshment and relaxation. If you're energetic, climb to the summit of Maki Hill for a great sunset view of the town and surroundings.
8:00 p.m.	Dine on the latest seafood catch at a restaurant on Russell's Strand. Sleep well in the Russell area.

Orientation

For touring purposes the Northland region can be divided into four areas: the coast east of Highway 1 to the Bay of Islands; the Bay of Islands northward to Doubtless Bay; Kaitaia and Cape Reinga; and the west coast from Aupori at the base of 90 Mile Beach to Kaipara Harbour. The Northland Peninsula stretches 280 miles from Auckland to the tip of Cape Reinga. Including lunch and rest stops, without side-trips, it's a ten-hour drive one-way. Russell in the Bay of Islands is no less than a five-hour drive. With only three days in the Northland, concentrate your sightseeing in the Bay of Islands region and on the west coast.

The Bay of Islands is the birthplace of modern New

Zealand's history. The Treaty of Waitangi, establishing
British rule, was signed there on 6 February, 1840.
Fascinating links with the country's past will be found in
Russell, on Waitangi Peninsula, and in Kerikeri. Visit sites of
conflict, struggle and habitation of Maoris, whalers, British
soldiers and civil government, missionaries and early settlers,
now embedded in tranquillity and natural beauty.

The Bay of Islands consists of three resort areas: Paihia, the
commercial, accommodation and excursion centre; Russell,
historic and fishing charter centre; and Kerikeri, a scenic
citrus-growing and historic centre. Except for Paihia, a very
popular Kiwi holiday resort area especially during Christmas
and the January school holiday period, the region is not
commercial and is protected by the Bay of Islands Maritime
and Historic Park.

The Bay of Islands Maritime and Historic Park
Headquarters (tel. 37-685) on the Strand in Russell should be
the first stop, especially for anyone planning to cruise, sail,
fish, ramble or camp in the park. Upon arrival in Paihia, stop
at the Public Relations Office on the waterfront.

On the way to Russell and the Bay of Islands

Highway 1 up the east side of the Peninsula is the fastest
route to the Bay of Islands. Highway 1 passes through rolling
hill country with pastoral pockets of green flat land. At one
time the entire region was covered by kauri, which has
disappeared to be replaced by sheep and dairy livestock
grazing. Virtually every town you'll see began as a timber
town for cutting, milling or shipping kauri or for the digging
of kauri gum. From 1853 to 1910, kauri gum was the
second most valuable export from the region—after kauri
timber.

The east coast is a constant variety of forms. The sandy
crescents of Pakiri and Bream Bay are small safe harbours
tucked into small bays between major peninsulas like
Whangaparoa and Whangarei Heads, and the large deep-water
inlet at Whangarei. On the drive north you'll pass
Wenderholm Regional Park, where beautiful groves of trees
on rolling hills are a backdrop to the beach. Pick up some
fresh fruit at the fruit stalls of family orchards on the road to
Warkworth before turning off to Sandspit for the ferry to
Kawau Island.

Lovers of superb coastal scenery should follow the
suggested schedule and take one or more detours: to Kawau
Island from Sandspit (east of Warkworth); to Mangawhai
Heads and the Mangawhai Walkway, and north through

Waipu Cove (about 60 miles); through Whangarei to
Whangarei Heads and Ocean Beach (about 22 miles); or along
the Tutukaka Coast (about 48 miles), with access to great
diving around the Poor Knights Islands.

Transport

The Northland is small enough to be covered by car in a few
days, though for sailors, divers, deep-sea fishing and walking
enthusiasts it deserves at least a week. I prefer driving to the
Northland for several reasons. It enables you to take several
coastal side-trips south and north of Whangarei. But services
from the Bay of Islands to the west coast are infrequent, and
without a car it is difficult to schedule visits to the Waipoua
State Forest, Trounson Kauri Park, Kai-Iwi Lakes and
Matakohe's museum. Bus transport to the Coromandel
Peninsula from Auckland runs infrequently and is difficult to
time with the departure from Northland, although you could
stay overnight in Auckland and head for Thames the next
morning.

On the other hand, you really don't need a car in the Bay of
Islands. Motorcoaches and buses connect Auckland with all
major Northland attractions and the Bay of Islands with
Dargaville. The NZRR runs daily coaches from Auckland,
departing at 8:45 a.m. through Whangarei (noon arrival) to
Paihia at 1:40 p.m., fare NZ$21 (£8.50) single. Newmans
Coach Lines (205 Hobson Street) departs Auckland at 5:00
p.m. daily and 9:00 a.m. on Saturday, NZ$17 (£6.50) single.

Paihia, Russell, Waitangi and Kerikeri should be seen on
foot. Minibuses can take you from Paihia to anywhere in the
area. If you wind up on the wrong side of the water at night,
it's an expensive mistake (how expensive depends on the
number of people, time of night and season) but not fatal.
Just call Bay Water Taxi (tel. 27-221) or Think Pink Water
Taxi Service (tel. 27-161). A 15-minute ferry runs regularly
between Paihia and Russell (NZ$3.25 (£1.30) adult return).
Three miles south of Paihia, at Opua, a boat charter harbour,
an inexpensive car ferry (car and two people NZ$4.50 (£1.80)
single) crosses the channel to Okiato Point, five miles from
Russell. The last car ferry from Opua to Russell departs at
7:00 p.m. most nights except Friday, and later in the summer
months.

Besides Russell's charm, Waitangi's historic sites, views and
golf course and picturesque Kerikeri, enjoying the other
sightseeing attractions in the Bay of Islands requires a launch
cruise, boat charter or, as a last expensive resort, hiring a
water taxi.

Sightseeing highlights

● ●**Kawau Island,** part of the Hauraki Gulf Maritime Park, is reached by ferry from Sandspit. Ferries (tel. 0846-8006) depart at 10:30 a.m. or noon, and return around 3:30 p.m., NZ$14 (£5.60) adult, NZ$7 (£2.50) child. Kawau Island was purchased (1862) and transformed into a subtropical delight of imported trees, plants and animals, including wallabies and kookaburras, by Sir George Grey, one of New Zealand's mid-19th century governors. The Governor's restored Mansion House and gardens are open daily from 9:30 a.m. to 3:30 p.m. Also see the cottages and mineshafts (copper and manganese) dating from the 1830s.

●**Mangawhai Cliffs Track,** a three-mile walkway near Mangawhai Heads, requires strong shoes for the rocky coast. The walk leads along cliff tops with a magnificent seascape on one side and vistas of green hills on the other.

●**Whangarei Falls** drop 75 feet into a green pool surrounded by luxuriant bush. With walkways above and below, it's a photographer's paradise. Visit the falls on the way to Tutukaka, taking Ngunguru Road.

● ● ●**The Bay of Islands Maritime and Historic Park** extends from Whangaroa Harbour to the north to Whangauru Harbour in the south, including 54 reserves of which 15 are offshore islands.

● ● ●**Russell,** a wild whaling port (Kororareka) in the early 1800s, later a British settlement and scene of British-Maori conflict, today is a charming historic town. One of the first stops should be the Bay of Islands Maritime and Historic Park Headquarters on the waterfront, the Strand, for free information and informative audiovisual displays. The park ranger can tell you everything you want to know about hiking, fishing and camping and also issues camping permits. Along the waterfront, the Duke of Marlborough Hotel was one of Kororareka's most popular drinking spots, and holds New Zealand's customs house. At the southern end of the Strand stands the impressive Pompellier House, named after a Bishop (who didn't actually live there), open 10:00 a.m. to 12:30 p.m. and 1:30 p.m. to 4:30 p.m., NZ$2.75 (£1.10) adult and NZ$.70 (£0.28) child (tel. 37-861). The oldest surviving church in New Zealand, Christ Church, is nearby. The Captain Cook Memorial Museum, York Street (tel. 37-701), displays many relics of early town life and a 21-foot replica of Captain Cook's *Endeavour*. The museum is open daily from 10:00 a.m. to 4:00 p.m., NZ1.65 (£0.66) adult and NZ$.20 (£0.08) child.

Right from the boat ramp end of the Strand, it's a
30-minute climb up historic Maki Hill (also known as
Flagstaff Hill) for a panoramic view of the town and the Bay
of Islands.

Where to eat

En route to Russell from Auckland, if you're too hungry to
drive any further, stop at **Ferryman's**, tel. 27-515, on the
Opua ferry wharf for smoked marlin, or fresh local crayfish
live from the tank. The setting, inside and outside, is perfect
for seafood meals.

In Russell, the **Holiday Village Inn**, Chapel Street, tel.
37-640, has a well-deserved reputation for big, delicious and
inexpensive meals. Otherwise, the small group of local
restaurants is much more expensive but offers the best food
and selection in the Bay of Islands.

For some of the freshest fish you've ever tasted, heaps of
shrimp cocktail or steak dishes, except on Sunday, try the
Reef Bar Bistro, tel. 37-831, in the Duke Tavern. Next
door, the **Duke of Marlborough** is very pricey dining in
elegant surroundings, but their five-course lunch is good
value. **The Gables**, tel. 37-618, on the waterfront is
moderately expensive but, with its very tasteful and
comfortable early colonial decor, well worth a smoked marlin
with avocado preceded by creamy oyster or mussel chowder
and topped off with their chocolate mocha mousse.

Where to stay

If you plan to visit the Bay of Islands during peak summer
months (15 December to the end of January) or school
holidays, be sure to book well in advance through the Public
Relations Office, P.O. Box 70, Paihia, tel. 27-426, open 8:30
a.m. to 5:30 p.m. Rates go up during these periods, too.

Wairoro Park, three fully equipped A-frame chalets and a
cabin, about a mile from the Opua car ferry, on 160 acres in a
beautiful setting on the shores of a cove, is highly
recommended for families and groups, with rates starting at
NZ$50 (£20) double, tel. 37-255. The **Arcadia Lodge**,
Florence Avenue, tel. 37-756, with four attractive,
comfortable, fully equipped and relatively inexpensive cabins,
also has great views of the Bay. Doubles start at NZ$36
(£14.50).

Russell Motor Camp, Longbeach Road, tel. 37-826, has
campsites (NZ$6 (£2.40) per night per person), caravan sites
(NZ$5.50 (£2.20) per person) and cabins (NZ$30 (£12)).
Brumby Farm Family Caravan Park, tel. 37-704, on the

Opua car ferry road has camping sites (NZ$8 (£3.20)
minimum) and cabins (NZ$25 (£10)). Campers should book
at the Park Headquarters in Russell, take a water taxi and
head for the beautiful Ranfurly Bay Reserve Park hut at the
entrance to Whangaroa Harbour.

The **Motel Russell**, Matauwhi Bay Road, tel. 37-854, has
13 very comfortable rooms, all with kitchens, in a wooded
hillside location. Doubles start at NZ$50 (£20). New
Zealand's first hotel, **The Duke of Marlborough**, The
Strand, tel. 37-829, is cosy in an old-world way, well worth
the NZ$70 (£28) rate for a double. The next best thing to
staying overnight is joining the lively conversation at the
Duke's pub or enjoying the fare in its fine dining room.

Alternative accommodation

In the event that accommodation in Russell is full or not
available in the right price range, here are some alternatives in
Paihia and Waitangi.

Backpackers will find a comfortable and clean place to stay
for NZ$7 (£2.80) per person in four flats holding 36 people at
the **Centabay Travellers' Hostel**, Selwyn Road, tel. 27-466,
for NZ$11 (£4.40) per person. **The Lodge**, Ivanhoe,
Puketona Road, tel. 27-466, also caters to backpackers with
dorm-style accommodation at NZ$6 (£2.40). Secluded in a
sheltered bay over a mile outside Paihia toward Opua is
Smiths Holiday Camp, tel. 27-678, with relatively
inexpensive self-contained motel units at NZ$32 (£13) double
and one room to de-luxe cabins from NZ$20 (£8) double.

In the opposite direction, **Twin Pines Motor Camp**,
Puketona Road, tel. 27-322, north of Paihia overlooking
Haruru Falls, has caravan sites, cabins, hostels, and motel flats
ranging from NZ$6 (£2.40) per adult to NZ$35 (£14) for two
people. Almost four miles from Paihia past Haruru Falls, **The
Lily Pond Holiday Park**, Puketona Road, tel. 27-646, offers
some of the best deals in town for camping, caravan sites and
11 cabins, ranging from NZ$6 (£2.40) to NZ$25 (£10). **The
River Park Motor Camp**, tel. 27-525, along the Waitangi
with a great view of Haruru Falls, is also excellent value for
camping and caravaning at NZ$5.50 (£2.20) per person. The
Mayfair Lodge, Puketona Road, tel. 27-471, offers bunk-bed
dormitory rooms for NZ$11 (£4.40) per person.

Ideal for families are the spotless, nicely furnished,
reasonably priced rooms with every needed facility, service
and amenity at the **Bay of Islands Motel**, Te Haumi,
Tohitapu Road, tel. 27-348, the **Casa-Bella Motel**,
McMurray Road, tel. 27-387, the **Aywon Motel**, Davis

Crescent, tel. 27-684, and the **Ala-Moana Motel**, Marsden
Road, tel. 27-745, with singles from NZ$30–$48 (£12–£19)
and doubles NZ$42–$55 (£17–£22). The **THC Waitangi**,
tel. 27-411, on the magnificent Waitangi Peninsula, costs
about NZ$80 (£32) per day for two.

Itinerary options

There's a one-way or return cruise with marvellous coastal
scenery from Auckland to Kawau Island, then on to Cape
Brett and Russell in the Bay of Islands, and through the Bay
of Islands Maritime and Historic Park to Whangaroa. Check
on the Explorer cruise offered by the NZ Adventure Centre,
costing NZ$175–$500 (£70–£200) return per person.

For those in a hurry, Mount Cook Airlines has three flights
a day Monday to Saturday and one flight on Sunday to
Kerikeri with a connecting motorcoach to Paihia. Sea Bee Air
offers regular flights to Paihia.

The Clapham Clock Museum (tel. 71-384) in Water Street
in Whangarei contains about 1,000 varieties of clocks and
watches. Open Monday to Friday 10 a.m. to 4:00 p.m., 3:00
p.m. at weekends.

Tutukaka Coast is a favourite deep-sea fishing base. For all
information, check at the Whangarei Deep Sea Anglers Club
at the marina. The eight miles of coastline between Ngunguru
and Sandy Bay are especially good for surfing. A short trail
through the woods reaches the splendid Whale Bay.

The Poor Knights Islands, off the Tutukaka Coast, are
world famous for diving and underwater photography. The
sub-tropical waters in this area offer rich havens of colourful
underwater life, with many school fish, large reef fish, and
steep drop-offs covered in brilliantly coloured anemones and
sponges. The best time for scuba diving is January to May.
October to December the visibility is poor. All necessary
information, equipment and charters can be arranged with the
Tutukaka Dive Shop or the Whangarei Deep Sea Anglers
Club. From Tutukaka's marina, take a skin-diving or
underwater photography trip to the Poor Knight Islands.

TOUR 5

RUSSELL—BAY OF ISLANDS—
WAITANGI—KERIKERI

Take a leisurely cruise from Russell to islands in the Bay of
Islands Maritime and Historic Park. In the afternoon, leave
Russell the same way you came, by the Opua Ferry, then
drive through Paihia to the historic Waitangi Peninsula. Visit
the Treaty House and the nearby Maori meeting house and
kauri war canoe. Drive to the beautiful Haruru Falls on the
way to Kerikeri. Explore Kerikeri Inlet until the sunset is
gone and it's time for dinner at the Stone Store Restaurant.

Suggested schedule

8:00 a.m.	Breakfast, local sightseeing and check out.
10:00 a.m.	Depart on the Cream Trip.
12:00 noon	Picnic lunch at Otehei Bay on Urupukapuka Island.
1:30 p.m.	Return to Russell.
2:00 p.m.	Depart from Russell via the Opua car ferry and then drive through Paihia to the Waitangi Peninsula. Visit the Treaty House and other historic sites.
4:00 p.m.	Depart from Waitangi and pass Haruru Falls on the way to Kerikeri. Check in upon arrival.
6:00 p.m.	Explore Kerikeri Inlet until sunset.
8:00 p.m.	Dinner at the Stone Store Restaurant, quiet relaxation and overnight in Kerikeri.

Sightseeing highlights
●●●**The Cream Trip** is one of the best ways, short of
having your own cruiser or yacht, to see the Bay of Islands.
It's named after a coastal launch route of the 1920s that
collected cream and delivered mail and supplies to dairy
farms. Fullers Cruises (tel. 27-421) operates the boat from
Paihia (9:45 a.m. daily) and Russell (10:00 a.m. daily) to many
islands, delivering mail and groceries to farmers and
caretakers on Monday, Wednesday and Friday. The four-hour
trip includes a lunch stop at Otehei Bay on Urupukapuka
Island. Lunch and the cruise costs NZ$40 (£16). (Note: you

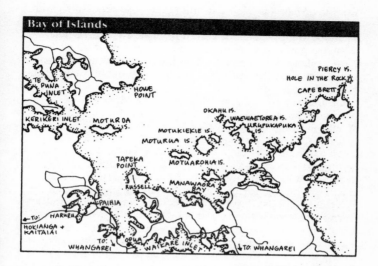

Bay of Islands

can camp free almost anywhere on Urupukapuka Island and use the Cream Trip as your transport to the island. Get the 'Urupukapuka Island Campers' brochure at the park headquarters in Russell.) Fullers also has several other cruises.

●**Paihia** is jammed with motels and hotels, but the town centre at the waterfront and wharf still has the character of a deep-sea fishing centre for dozens of local game-fishing boats. Look for crowds around the wharf as a sign that a magnificent game fish is being weighed in. The Fullers and Mt. Cook cruises, as well as most other sightseeing cruises and charters, leave from Paihia's wharf.

●●●**The Waitangi National Reserve** on Waitangi Peninsula, only a mile from Paihia, is one of the most historic places in New Zealand. On 6 February, 1840, the Treaty of Waitangi was signed on the lawn in front of the home of the first British Resident, James Busby. Local Maori chiefs, fearing the takeover of their land by France or other foreign countries, had asked for British protection. Over 2,000 Maoris assembled there to meet Captain Hobson, who informed them that Queen Victoria would offer such protection under a treaty in return for ceding sovereignty to the Crown. With much opposition, which persists to this day, the treaty was signed and, on 8 February, the British Colony of New Zealand was proclaimed with the hoisting of flags and a 21-gun salute. Nearby is the Waitangi Meeting House, a gift

from the Maoris to New Zealand at the 1940 centennial, with
wall carvings from many North Island tribes. Also nearby is a
118-foot Maori war canoe carved from kauri. The 18-hole
Waitangi golf course is one of the finest and most scenic in
New Zealand. Drive around it on the road that climbs nearly
to the top of Mt. Bledisloe for the best panoramic views of the
Bay of Islands.

On the way to Waitangi, stop off at the **Museum of
Shipwrecks**, a three-masted barque moored near the
Waitangi-Paihia bridge holding a collection of diver Kelley
Tarlton's salvage from local shipwrecks. Afterwards, walk or
drive to **Haruru Falls**, a beautiful waterfall in a very lovely
setting for a swim in the estuary of the Waitangi River
surrounded by native trees. The falls, which are floodlit at
night, can be reached by a 3.6-mile walking track through the
Waitangi National Reserve or by driving less than two miles
inland along the road to Puketona. The falls are also a
beautiful spot for swimming in the estuary. While in the
vicinity, consider having a snack lunch at the Dewdrop Bar or
dining upstairs at Goffes Restaurant on the upper floor of
Twin Pines Tavern (tel. 27-195).

●●**Kerikeri**, founded in 1819 as a mission station, today is
known for its citrus fruit groves, large numbers of artists and
craftsmen, and two historic buildings in lovely Kerikeri
Basin—the Stone Store and Museum (1833), the oldest stone
building in New Zealand, and Kemp House (1822), probably
the oldest wooden building in the country. On the drive from
Paihia to Kerikeri, the road is lined with orchards of oranges,
mandarins, tangelos, kiwi fruit, tamarillos and feijoas,
sheltered behind hedgerows in the landscape around Kerikeri.
Approaching Kerikeri Basin, the red roof and white face of
the Kemp House, set above the stolid Stone House on the
shoreline, is a reminder that the 'Fruitbowl of the North' is
also a cradle of New Zealand's colonisation. The most
noteworthy and symbolic aspect of the Stone House is that it
was built by missionaries to withstand native attacks that
never occurred because of the humane and understanding way
in which the missionaries involved themselves with the
Maoris. Nearby is Rewi's Village, an accurate full-scale
reconstruction of a Maori *kainga* (unfortified village). A
walking track follows the river from the Ranger Station to the
spectacular **Rainbow Falls**, about 90 feet high. For fun try
the **Orchard Railway**, about half a mile of narrow track
with a small train running through gum trees and sub-tropical
orchards, ending at a restored country station.

Where to stay

The **Kerikeri Youth Hostel**, Main Road, tel. 79-391, on several acres just north of town, is within easy walking distance of river swimming and historic sites. Six dormitory rooms with 28 beds and a communal kitchen cost NZ$9 (£3.60) per person.

One of the prettiest sites for accommodation in the region belongs to the six chalet units of the **Riverview Chalets**, 28 Landing Road, tel. 78-741, on the river bank overlooking Stone House and Kemp House, from NZ$55–$65 (£22–£26) double. The **Spanish House Motel**, Inlet Road, tel. 79-311, 2½ miles from town on 13 acres of farmland, with panoramic views of Kerikeri Inlet, has NZ$45–$55 (£18–£22) singles or doubles.

Where to eat

Paihia has eating places of all sorts in proportion to its abundance of motels. The **Jolly Roger** in Kings Road, tel. 27-783, should take care of anyone's sit-down or take-away needs for shrimp, oysters, scallops and friendly service. Classic deep-fried dishes, local seafood and meat are prepared in different styles downstairs and upstairs at the popular **Bella Vista** on the waterfront, tel. 27-451, at the French provincial-style **Courtyard Restaurant**, Beachhaven Motel, Marsden Road, tel. 27-444, and at the more expensive **La Scala**, Selwyn Road Shopping Centre upstairs, tel. 27-031.

For the famished traveller, I highly recommend the **THC Waitangi**'s huge buffet lunch or Sunday brunch at the **Poolside Restaurant** (tel. 27-411). The grills and salads at the **Anchorage Grill** are plain and good. The hotel's **Governor's Room** is a budget-buster in the French tradition.

Jane's Restaurant, State Highway 10 between Paihia and Kerikeri, tel. 78-664, is a very cosy, relaxed place to have an early or late breakfast or a very good quality and moderately priced French provincial dinner, open seven nights a week. The tough competition in Kerikeri for Jane's is the BYO **Stone Store Restaurant**, tel. 78-194, located amid lawn and garden in the lovely Kerikeri Inlet, with an incredibly good, diverse and reasonably priced fish and meat menu.

Itinerary options

Mt. Cook's Tiger Lily Cruises, tel. 27-099, Cape Brett Hole in the Rock Cruise departs from Paihia at 9:30 a.m. and 1:00 p.m., returning at 12:30 and 4:00 p.m., and costs NZ$31 (£12.50) adult. The four-hour Super Cruise departs from

Paihia at 10:00 a.m. and returns at 2:00 p.m. The cruise visits
Cape Brett, Piercy Island, Cathedral Cave and the Hole in the
Rock at Cape Brett.

Join a skippered charter in Kerikeri for a day-trip along the
Kerikeri Inlet into the Bay of Islands and up the coast to the
Cavilli Islands and Whangaroa. High domed and craggy
volcanic hills surround Whangaroa's harbour, dotted with
small islands.

Golfers, visit the Kerikeri Golf Club, a championship
course, with facilities available to visitors.

Scenic flightseeing charters are available at the Kerikeri
Airport off Highway 10. The Bay of Islands Aero Club
operates high-wing aircraft for good visibility and
photography. Flights generally last from 20 minutes to two
hours.

Cruising or yachting, perhaps combined with diving, game
or light-tackle fishing, is the best way to experience the Bay of
Islands for those with the time and budget. **Rainbow Yacht
Charters** (Auckland: tel. 790-457; Opua: tel. 0885-27821)
offers the most complete skippered or bareboat sailing holiday
packages on a wide variety of yachts and motorcruisers.
Cruising and sailing instruction is required for those without
sufficient experience. Expect to spend from NZ$160 to
NZ$800 (£64–£320) per day, depending on the type of boat
and season, and roughly double that for skippered boats. Five
or six companions can bring down the cost per person. The
Northland Charter Boat Association in Russell and the
Game Fishing Charter Association in the Paihia Marine
Building offer fully equipped single or shared charters,
picking up people in Paihia, Russell or Waitangi at around
8:00 a.m., returning before 6:00 p.m.

Diving in the sub-tropical waters of the Bay of Islands,
around the Poor Knights Islands off the Tutukaka Coast or
the Three Kings Islands off the northern tip of Cape Reinga,
offers rich havens of colourful underwater life. Some of the
best diving areas are: Cathedral Cove almost splitting Piercy
Island; between Home Point and Cape Wiwiki on the Purerua
Peninsula east of Kerikeri; around Dog Island; Bird Rock and
Twins Rock; Hope Reef in the Albert Channel off
Urupukapuka; Paramena Reef in Te Uenga Bay; Whale Rock
northwest of Okahu Island; Waewaetorea, Takarota Rock
between Motutakapu and Nakataunga, and Tokananohia Reef.
A seven-hour diving trip with **Paihia Dive and Fishing
Trips**, including all equipment, costs about NZ$100 (£40)
per person.

TOUR 6

BAY OF ISLANDS—COROMANDEL PENINSULA

Leave the Bay of Islands heading for the west coast of Northland, then south to visit the Waipoua Kauri Sanctuary on the way to Dargaville. Visit two exceptional regional museums, in Dargaville and Matakohe, before continuing south past Auckland to Thames on the Coromandel Peninsula.

Suggested schedule

7:00 a.m.	Breakfast in Kerikeri.
8:00 a.m.	Depart for west coast.
11:00 a.m.	Waipoua Kauri Sanctuary.
12:30 p.m.	Picnic lunch on the West Coast Beach adjoining Dargaville.
1:30 p.m.	Visit Dargaville regional museum.
3:00 p.m.	Otamatea Kauri and Pioneer Museum in Matakohe.
4:00 p.m.	Leave for final leg of trip to Coromandel Peninsula.
8:30 p.m.	Arrive in Thames, Coromandel Peninsula.
9:00 p.m.	Late dinner and a waterfront stroll before retiring.

Driving to the west coast, Auckland and Thames

Go west from Kerikeri on Highway 12 to Opononi via Rawene (about 1½ hours' drive). From there, continuing on Highway 12 through the Waipoua Kauri Forest and by Trounson Kauri Park to Dargaville, is less than two hours without stops. Follow Highway 12 through Matakohe to Highway 1 south. From Dargaville to Highway 1 is also less than two hours; allow about a half an hour at the Dargaville Museum and about 45 minutes at the museum in Matakohe. From Wellsford on Highway 1 it's 1½ hours to Auckland. You should pass Auckland at about 6:00 p.m. It's about an hour on Highway 1 from Auckland to just before Pokeno, where you turn east for another hour on Highway 2 to Kopu, a few miles south of Thames. Turn north on Route 26 to Thames.

Sightseeing highlights

● ● ●**The Waipoua Kauri Forest** contains some of the
best specimens of the North Island's once vast forests of giant
kauri trees. The Northland's early history was very much
shaped by the presence of these aged giants, first cut at a
frenzied pace for local use and export as ship's masts and
building material. Then the resinous kauri gum was dug from
the ground by thousands of Yugoslavian diggers for export to
the United States and Europe to make varnish. In just a few
decades of the early 19th century, kauri forests were reduced
to small scattered stands. Rivalling California redwoods in
height (170 ft.), girth (50 ft.) and age (some as old as 2000
years), kauris can be seen in two forests east of Highway 12
north of Dargaville: **Waipoua Forest Sanctuary** and
Trounson Kauri Park, located about nine miles south of
Waipoua (including a few campsites). The Waipoua Forestry
Headquarters (tel. Donnelly's Crossing 605) is on Highway 12
at the southern end of the forest.

● ●**Regional museums** at Dargaville and Matakohe, as well
as Russell and Kaitaia, contain extensive material on the
'Kauri Era'. The **Otamatea Kauri and Pioneer Museum**
(tel. 37-417) in Matakohe has a unique kauri gum collection
and the kauri gum story is told with photographs, models,
early furniture, industrial tools and more. Open daily 9:00
a.m. to 5:00 p.m.

●**Dargaville**, a thriving port during the kauri timber and
gum era, has the **Northern Wairoa Maori, Maritime and
Pioneer Museum** housing pre-European Maori, kauri and
maritime sections. Open daily, except Saturday, 2:00 to 4:00
p.m. only. West of Dargaville, stretching from Kaipara Head
north to Maunganui Bluffs, is the Northland's longest ocean
beach (68 miles), the West Coast Beach, with black iron sand
typical of Tasman Sea beaches.

Where to stay

There is a good choice of motor camps in the Thames area,
including **Dickson Park Motor Camp**, Victoria Street,
Teraru, tel. 87-308, **Boomerang Motor Camp**, Coromandel
Road, Te Puru, tel. 78-879, and **Waiomu Bay Motor
Camp**, Highway 25, tel. Te Puru 78-777. North of
Coromandel are the **Angler's Lodge and Motor Park,
Coromandel Motel & Caravan Park**, and the **Oamaru
Park Tourist Flats and Caravan Park**, all offering caravan
sites, on-site vans, tourist cabins and in some instances tourist
flats and motel rooms.

There are five hotels in Thames—the **Brian Boru Hotel**, Pollen Street, tel. 86-523, **Imperial**, 476 Pollen Street, tel. 86-200, **Junction Hotel**, Pollen Street, tel. 86-908, **Salutation Hotel**, 400 Mary Street, tel. 86-488, and **Warwick Arms**, Pollen Street, tel. 86-183. They range in price from NZ$20 to NZ$40 (£8–£16) singles and doubles. The **Brian Boru**, built in 1868, is the most exceptional (and expensive), especially its two-day Agatha Christie Weekends, which combine rafting, a beach trip, wine tasting, two-nights' lodging, sumptuous breakfasts, supper and buffet dinner, and a fun 'whodunnit' involving 30 guests and eight actors, for NZ$300 (£120) per person.

The Thames area has about a dozen very good small motels that offer most amenities including kitchens for NZ$35–$55 (£14–£22) per night single. The **Puru Park Motel**, Puru Bay, tel. 84-378, is the top of the group. The **Motel Rendezvous**, Highway 25 at Kopu, tel. 88-536, at NZ$32 (£13) single is the most reasonable.

Where to eat

In Thames, the **Brian Boru Hotel**, tel. 86-523, serves excellent bistro lunches and Sunday night smorgasbord, 5:00 to 8:00 p.m.

Except for the Brian Boru, save your dining money for the Aorangi Peak or Rumours in Rotorua (Tour 7 or Tour 8). Check on Pollen Street in Thames for a variety of eateries. The **Hotel Imperial** will do nicely for reasonably tasty and moderately priced counter meals and more expensive (but not outstanding) cuisine in the **Regency Room**. Down the street, the **Pizza Cabin**, 702 Pollen Street, is not what you think with its diverse and inexpensive menu ranging from pizza to delicious Bluff oysters, steak and other dishes.

The **Bakehouse** in Wharf Road in Coromandel, with its delicious bread and baked goods, is an excellent place to pick up ingredients for a picnic lunch tomorrow.

Itinerary options

Kai-Iwi Lakes, three relatively unspoiled lakes about 19 miles north of Dargaville, deserve a side trip on the way south to Dargaville for trout fishing, swimming and walking. From Highway 12 at Maropui, turn west along Omamari Road to the end, then right onto Kai-Iwi Lakes Road, then right along Domain Road to Taharoa Domain. The white sand beach on this beautiful lake is a perfect stop for swimming or fishing before continuing to Auckland and Coromandel. Taharoa Domain also offers lakeside camping.

TOUR 7

COROMANDEL PENINSULA— ROTORUA

Make a partial circuit of the west and east Coromandel Peninsula coastlines, then follow the Bay of Plenty through Tauranga and Mt. Maunganui before turning south to the Rorotua Lake and thermal region.

Suggested schedule

8:00 a.m.	After breakfast, head north to Coromandel.
10:00 a.m.	Visit Coromandel.
12:00 noon	Take Highway 309 to the east coast for a picnic lunch on Hot Water Beach.
1:30 p.m.	Drive south to Tauranga on the Bay of Plenty.
5:00 p.m.	Arrive in Tauranga and take a possible side trip to Mount Maunganui.
8:30 p.m.	Arrive in Rotorua, check in and enjoy a thermal bath before a late dinner.

Driving from Coromandel to Rotorua

Just 75 miles south-east of Auckland, the Coromandel Peninsula's volcanic mountains and rugged coastal scenery jut out between the Hauraki Gulf and the Bay of Plenty. A car is necessary on the Peninsula. The Auckland Railways Road Service's coaches travel between Auckland and Thames, but otherwise bus services are limited to Thames, Coromandel and Whitianga on the Bay of Plenty.

Leaving Auckland on Highways 1 and then 2, the drive along the connecting Highway 25 is lush and scenic. The route passes through rolling green farmland with few settlements. Just a few miles past Mangatawhiri, the road branches to the left toward the extensive vineyards of Mangatangi. The pine forest south of Highway 2, planted by the New Zealand government, can be used for recreation. Route 25 from Thames to Coromandel is surfaced, as is Route 25 from Whitianga south to the Bay of Plenty. Otherwise, most of the roads on the Peninsula are loose gravel and slow going. Take Highway 25 from Thames to Coromandel along the Firth of Thames, then backtrack three miles to Highway 309, an unsurfaced winding road with spectacular views.

Continue south through Coroglen for about ten miles
watching for the turn-off to Hot Water Beach. A fork in the
road to Hot Water Beach leads to Hahei Beach.

After a beach stop, continue south on Highway 25 to Waihi
where it connects with Highway 2 south to Tauranga, Mt.
Maunganui and the turn-off to Highway 33 to Rotorua which
is a few miles past Te Puke. Highway 33 merges with
Highway 30 into Rotorua.

Orientation

Coromandel Peninsula is a nature lover's and sportsman's
paradise, sprinkled with reminders of the area's gold mining
and kauri milling days. Coastal roads follow a wonderfully
varied coastline, with side roads leading to some of New
Zealand's most scenic beaches. The forested Coromandel
Range is cut through by winding mountain and valley roads
connecting west and east coasts that offer several trip options,
such as the Kauaeranga Valley Road, the Tapu-Coroglen
Road and Highway 309. Mayor Island off the south-west
coast is the centre of deep-sea fishing activity. You'll arrive
too late to visit the Thames Information and PR Centre
(Queen Street, tel. 87-284). It's the first place to go in the
morning for information and maps.

Sightseeing highlights

● **Coromandel's Courthouse**, built in 1873 for the gold
warden 20 years after the discovery in Coromandel of the first
gold in New Zealand, now serves as the local Council
Chambers.

● ● **Highway 309**, a narrow and winding 'short-cut' across
the peninsula from Coromandel Harbour to Kaimarama, has
stunning scenery.

● ● **Mercury Bay to Waihi Beach** displays spectacular
headland and beach scenery, though it can be very crowded
during holiday periods. In this coastal stretch, stop off at
Hahai Beach, Hot Water Beach, Pauanui and Mount Paka. At
Opou, a turn-off to the left south of Hikuai, the Opoutere
Youth Hostel (tel. Whangamata 59-072) puts you within a
short walk of Opoutere Beach.

● ● **Hahei Beach** (pink sand) and **Hot Water Beach** are
beautiful beaches, quite different from one another. Within a
few hours of low tide, just dig a hole on Hot Water Beach
between the cliff and the large rock offshore to soak in your
own natural hot pool bath seeping through the sand. The
fabulous headland scenery, two *pa* (Maori village) sites,
nearby blow holes (seawater forced through holes in coastal

rocks) at the southern end of Hahei's pink sands and the huge
cavern at Cathedral Cove Reserve on the northern end make
this an unsurpassed beach break. Tent sites are available at
Hahei Tourist Park, in case you just can't leave.

● **Pauanui** holiday town nestles in the pines along a golden
beach.

● The twin-peaked **Mt. Paka** across the Tairua Harbour
from Pauanui is the site of an old *pa*, where earthworks rise
up from the sea over 500 feet.

● ● **The Bay of Plenty**—There are plenty of attractions to
keep you in the Bay of Plenty on the way to Rotorua: mild
climate, fine broad beaches, clear water, excellent game
fishing or diving near Mayor Island, and great bush walks
on the island, Tauranga's beautiful parks, 'The Mount'
with its magnificent views, natural hot saltwater pools, a
wonderful surf beach (Ocean Beach) and excellent white-water
rafting.

● **Mt. Maunganui**—This beach resort, reached by ferry on
the eastern shore of Tauranga's harbour, has a 760-foot
wooded peak that is worth the climb for outstanding views of
the sea, Matakana Island, Tauranga City and Harbour, and
the surf beach stretching for 12 miles south to Maketu's
headland.

Where to stay

The best value in Rotorua is: the dormitory rooms at the
YHA Hostel, corner of Eruera and Hinemary Streets, tel.
476-810, at NZ$11 (£4.40) per person; the serviced rooms
and cabins for NZ$8-$12 (£3.20–£4.80) at the **Ivanhoe
Tourist Lodge**, 54 Haupapa Street, tel. 86-985; and the
Waiteti Holiday Park, 14 Okona Crescent, Ngongotaha, tel.
74-749, for a variety of tent sites, caravan sites, bunkhouse
beds, tourist cabins and flats, all in a wooded riverbank setting
(with trout), at NZ$11–$32 (£4.40–£13) double. With its
charming and well-equipped cabins, **Rainbow & Fairy
Springs**, State Highway, tel. 581-887, is a perfect place for
families of any size to relax in a pretty setting outside town.
Rates per cabin range from NZ$15 to NZ$45 (£6–£18). Less
charming but cheaper are the **Cosy Cottage** cabins, tel.
83-793, starting at NZ$15 (£6) for two, and the **Rotorua
Thermal Motor Camp**, Old Taupo Road, tel. 86-385,
starting at NZ$22 (£9) double.

Couples hunting for homely, attractive, clean, friendly, and
comparatively inexpensive B&Bs with their own mineral pools
should book in advance at either **Morihana Guest House**,
20 Toko Street, tel. 88-511, or **Tresco Guest House**, 3 Toko

Street, tel. 89-611, for around NZ$25 (£10) per person or
NZ$34–$38 (£13.50–£15) per couple.

There are plenty of less expensive (NZ$28–$50 (£11–£20))
twin or double motel flats in Rotorua, such as the **Motel
McHale**, 281 Fenton Street, tel. 89-612, **Mayfair Motel
Flats**, 7 Arawa Street, tel. 80-436, and the **Victoria Motel**,
10 Victoria Street, tel. 84-039.

If you are looking for total comfort, service, all facilities
(freshwater, thermal/mineral and spa pools) and lovely
grounds, expect to pay upwards of NZ$50 (£20) double at,
for example, the **Fernleaf Motel**, 23 Toko Street, tel.
87-129, or the **South Pacific Motel**, 98 Lake Road, tel.
80-153.

The **THC Rotorua International**, Whakarewarewa, tel.
81-189, and the **Sheraton Rotorua**, Fenton Street, tel. 81-
139, share the honours for the premier address in Rotorua.
The latter has the edge for luxury accommodation, exterior
and interior design and decor, and health and fitness facilities.
Both hotels start at about NZ$140 (£56) for double rooms,
which is not bad for what you get.

Where to eat

The first priority for dining (or should I say feasting) in
Rotorua is a traditional Maori *hangi*. The carefully timed and
controlled steam oven cooking of lamb, pork, seafood,
vegetables, pumpkin and pudding has been perfected by large
hotels like the **Rotorua International**, tel. 81-189, the
Rotorua Travelodge, tel. 81-174, the **Tudor Towers
Restaurant**, tel. 81-285, in Government Gardens, and
Geyserland Motor Hotel.

Start your quest for good food, light meals, grills or counter
service on Arawa Street with fish and steaks at the upstairs
Palace Tavern and Friar Tuck, tel. 81-492, in Ye Olde
English Taven atmosphere; perhaps *coq au vin* at the French
provincial bistro, **Gourmet**, tel. 82-198; and, for pancake
fans, the **Pancake Parlour Restaurant**. Tutanekai Street
has a few local and tourist favourites; for game dishes, the
enormous portions at **Karl's Dining Room**, tel. 80-231;
roast beef and lamb, seafood and wild game at **The
Bushman's Hut**, tel. 83-285; a superb fixed-price lunch at
the **Gazebo**, tel. 81-911.

Cobb & Co., tel. 82-089, in the Grand Establishment in
Hinemoa Street, is reliable, from decor to relatively
inexpensive and satisfying food, and seven-days-a-week
service from 7:30 a.m. to 10:00 p.m.

If you're going to Ohinemutu Village, make reservations at

the **Lake Tavern Restaurant,** tel. 85-585, in a great old
building overlooking the lake. When visiting the Agrodome,
don't miss the **Agrodome Tea Room** for a savoury lunch
and excellent desserts. Sunday smorgasbord (6:00 p.m. to 9:00
p.m.) at the **Geyserland Hotel** while watching Whaka's
thermal activity is a special treat. The literal translation of
Whakarewarewa is 'to rise up', originally referring to the
uprising of a local Maori war party; today the name refers to
steam clouds gushing skyward at unpredictable intervals. A
dining highlight in Rotorua is **Aorangi Peak,** tel. 86-957,
(book in advance), over 1,000 feet up Mt. Ngongotaha. If the
view and the venison medallions don't leave you breathless,
the bill will. Otherwise, trek up to dance on Friday or
Saturday night and enjoy the cocktail bar.

Less expensive, without a mountaintop view but with better
cuisine and desserts, is **Rumours,** tel. 477-277, at 581
Pukuatua. Like Aorangi Peak, you may have to make
reservations even before leaving Auckland.

TOUR 8

ROTORUA—LAKE TAUPO

The region between Rotorua and Lake Taupo is crammed with so many things to see and do that visiting the best of it takes a full day and is worth every minute of it. The day starts early with stops at trout springs just outside Rotorua and thermal, Maori and other attractions in Rotorua. Move south after lunch through Waimangu and Waikato Valleys, sightseeing as you go, to Lake Taupo. Before the day is over you'll have seen hot water springs, eerie boiling mud pools, steaming silica terraces, the blue-green lake of Waimangu Cauldron, smouldering rocks, steaming bush and cliffs with hot water gurgling out of rock crevices.

Suggested schedule

7:00 a.m.	Rise early for a full day.
8:00 a.m.	Breakfast and check out.
9:00 a.m.	Rainbow and Fairy Springs.
10:30 a.m.	Whakarewarewa and the Maori Arts and Crafts Institute.
12:00 noon	Snack lunch at the Agrodome.
1:00 p.m.	Waimangu Thermal Valley.
3:30 p.m.	Huka Falls, Aratiatia Rapids and the Wairakei Geothermal Steam Power Station.
6:00 p.m.	Check in at Taupo accommodation and fish for trout in Lake Taupo while there's still light.
8:00 p.m.	Dinner followed by a lakefront stroll.

Orientation

Ancestors of the Maoris landed on the shores of the Bay of Plenty around 1340 AD and pushed inland to Lake Rotorua, the centre of a giant (150 mile long and 20 mile wide) thermal region. The natural wonders confirmed the phenomenal activities of the gods. The many lakes and the thermal activity supplied food and warmth. The result today is New Zealand's largest concentration of Maori culture, arts and crafts, in the midst of an extraordinary assortment of thermal sites, volcanic mountains and the world's best trout fishing.

To the south of Rotorua, the beautiful Waikato River flows placidly northward, with a brief intermission at Huka Falls. To the east of Rotorua is a collection of magnificent

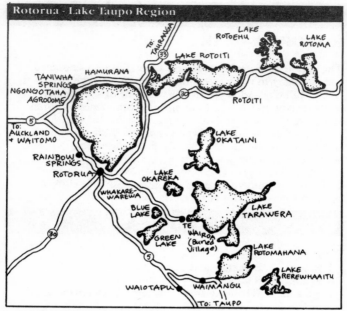

Rotorua - Lake Taupo Region

bush-fringed lakes and the Bay of Plenty, which is about the
same distance from Rotorua as Lake Taupo to the south. The
Bay of Plenty's waters teem with yellow fin and mako shark.
Fine beaches abound.

Sightseeing highlights

●●●**Rotorua** is 'Spa City', with over 600,000 visitors
annually. The resort hugs the south-western shore of Lake
Rotorua. The city's three primary attractions are
Whakarewarewa Thermal Reserve, the Maori Arts and Crafts
Institute, and Government Gardens.

●●●**Whakarewarewa Thermal Reserve** is the best place
in New Zealand to see many of the elements of living Maori
culture. Walk around the traditional village site,
Whakarewarewa, where carved meeting houses (*maraes*) and
huts are set among boiling pools and geysers. The local
Maoris still use thermal energy for cooking, washing and
heating. The Whakarewarewa thermal area is entered through
a replica of a fortified Maori village (*pa*) and ornately carved
gateway. Steaming cracks, boiling mud, silica terraces and
small geysers lead to Pohutu Geyser, New Zealand's highest
(100 ft.), with erratic bursts of boiling water and steam

clouds. Open daily from 8:30 a.m. to 4:30 p.m.

●●●**The New Zealand Maori Arts and Crafts
Institute**, outside the main entrance to Whakarewarewa, is
the training centre for Maori wood carvers. Maori flax
weaving techniques are demonstrated there as well. Open 8:30
a.m. to 4:30 p.m.

●●**Government Gardens** and its Elizabethan-style **Tudor
Towers**, built as a bath house in 1906-7 and restored by the
city, houses the Rotorua Museum and Art Gallery, the Fleur
International Orchid Gardens, the Rotorua Cricket Club, The
Sportsdrome (a new sports centre), Polynesian Pools and
thermal waters of varying mineral content and temperature.
Pool hours are 9:00 a.m. to 10:00 p.m., NZ$5.50 (£2.20) per
person.

●●**Rainbow and Fairy Springs** (tel. 81-887) combine
beautiful bush growth, pools full of rainbow and brown trout
viewed above and below water, and a variety of other
attractions. Open 8:00 a.m. to 5:00 p.m. To see more trout
pools in equally beautiful settings, continue north on Highway
5 to Taniwha Springs and Hamurana Springs.

●**The Agrodome** (tel. 74-350), seven miles from Rotorua,
offers three shows daily (9:15 a.m., 11:00 a.m. and 2:30 p.m.)
with a 60-minute demonstration of sheep shearing and the use
of sheep dogs. Combine the show with lunch at the Agrodome
Tea Room. NZ$3.50 (£1.40) per person.

●●**Ohinemutu** is an unusual Maori village with both the
Tamatekapua Meeting House and Tudor-style Maori
Anglican St. Faith's Church (with Maori carvings). The two
structures have faced each other for generations next to Lake
Rotorua. There are Maori concerts every night in summer at
the Ohinemutu meeting house (8:00 p.m., tel. 82-269).

●●**Ngongotaha**, three miles west on Highway 5, has natural
pools filled with thousands of rainbow, brown and brook trout
amidst 30 acres of natural growth, including Rainbow and
Fairy Springs, a bird aviary, nocturnal kiwis and a deer farm.
Drive up Mount Ngongotaha to the Aorangi Peak Restaurant
for a breathtaking panorama.

●●●**Maori** *hangi*, a Polynesian feast traditionally
steam-cooked in an underground pit, includes chicken, pork,
seafood, fish and other basics and delicacies and, after dinner,
a Maori concert. *Hangis* are put on at several hotels around
town for about NZ$18 (£7) per person. The THC
International Hotel traditionally has had the best one.

En route to Taupo

Taupo is a 1½ hour (50-mile) drive from Rotorua on

Highway 1. About 12 miles from Taupo, shortly before
Wairakei, is the turn-off to Aratiatia Rapids and Huka Falls.
Wairakei means 'Waters of Adorning', an apt name for this
geothermal area. Huka means 'foaming' which also describes
the sight of the blue-green Waikato River plunging through a
narrow cleft of rock.
● ●**Huka Falls** are not high, but the Waikato River
funnelling powerfully through a narrow gorge near Taupo
catapults the water over the ledge into the calm pool below.
● ●**Aratiatia Rapids** are about two miles from Highway 5,
just north of its intersection with Highway 1. The rapids flow
through a deep, rocky ravine to a small spillway and hydro-
electric power station at the head of the rapids on the Waikato
River downstream from Lake Taupo. Millions of native plants
have been planted in the area around the rapids. Water is
released over the dam from 10:00 to 11:30 a.m. and 2:30 to
4:00 p.m. daily.
● ● ●**Waimangu Thermal Valley** contains Waimangu
Cauldron, one of the world's largest boiling lakes. Walk past
the bubbling crater lake to the shores of Lake Rotomahana,
where a launch takes you to the Steaming Cliffs and site of
the former Pink and White Terraces. The devastating
eruption of Mount Tarawera, on 10 June, 1886, is said to
have been foretold by the appearance of a phantom war canoe
paddling across Lake Tarawera ten days before the eruption.
Several villages were completely destroyed, including Te
Wairoa, a busy centre for trips to the world famous Pink and
White Terraces of Lake Rotomahana. The three truncated
peaks of Mt. Tarawera, across Lake Tarawera, a short
distance from Te Wairoa, are still devoid of vegetation, an
ominous reminder of the disaster that occurred only a moment
ago in geological time. Visit the buried village of Te Wairoa,
Blue and Green Lakes and the Waiotapu thermal area
containing the Lady Knox Geyser that erupts daily at 10:15
a.m. to a height of 60 feet. See the Bridal Veil Falls cascade
over tinted silica terraces changing colours from white
through deep red and lemon to emerald green. NZ$5.50
(£2.20) adult, NZ$2.50 (£1) child, with an extra charge of
NZ$5 (£2) (NZ$3 (£1.20) child) for the launch ride. This
tour is covered by a full-day's NZRR excursion for NZ$24
(£9.50).
●**The Wairakei Geothermal Steam Power Station**, 50
miles south of Rotorua between Huka Falls and the Aratiatia
rapids, generates billows of clouds over an interesting energy
project. Take the walkway from Huka Falls to Aratiatia
through wild flowers in season.

●●**Lake Taupo** fills a gigantic (238-square-mile) crater. One
of the biggest volcanic eruptions in history, greater than
Krakatoa and Mt. St. Helens combined, devastated the region
1800 years ago. Today Lake Taupo is the trout fishing capital
of the world. About 100 years ago, trout eggs were brought
from California to what turned out to be perfect breeding
grounds at Lake Taupo. Fishing in the sparkling clear lake
waters, at the mouths of streams flowing into the lake from
the Kaimanawa Mountains or in the trout-pools of the famed
glacier-fed Tongariro River yields legendary rainbow (3-6
lbs.) and brown trout (5 lbs. and over) from April to August
during spawning runs. Lake Taupo also offers superb
water-skiing, pleasure boating and swimming.

Where to stay

Thanks to thousands of beds in the Taupo area, many in very
decent, inexpensive motel flats and two- to five-berth
furnished cabins, even hoards of fishermen at holiday times
shouldn't cause a serious problem. The Public Relations
Office, tel. 89-002, near the lakefront, can take care of your
accommodation and other needs. For around NZ$16-$22
(£6.50–£9) per night for two people, the **Acacia Holiday
Park**, Acacia Bay Road, tel. 85-159, the **Waitahanui**, tel.
87-183, and **Taupo Cabins**, 50 Tonga Street, tel. 84-346, are
sure winners.

The next level of accommodation is motel flats in the
NZ$35–$45 (£14–£18) range for doubles: **Acapulco**, tel.
87-174, **Dunrovin Motel**, 140 Heuheu Street, tel. 87-384,
and **Motel Taupo**, Four Mile Bay, tel. 85-992. The local
PRO knows many others.

There are many more good choices for NZ$40–$60
(£16–£24) double: **Adelphi Motel**, Heuheu Street, tel.
87-569, **Birchlands Motel**, 120 Robert Street, tel. 88-569,
Continental Motel, 9 Scannell Street, tel. 88-398, **De Brett
Thermal Motel**, Napier Highway, tel. 87-080, **Guestward
Ho Motel**, 9 Tui Street, tel. 87-487, **Lynwood Lodge**, tel.
84-967, **Motel Trianon**, 63 Mere Road, tel. 84-222,
Shoreline Motel, Waitahanui, tel. 86-912, and many other
relatively new ones.

Where to eat

Taupo is not a fancy resort, but large numbers of
holidaymakers all year round from around the world, who
come for the spectacular lake fishing and views, have ensured
that there is quality eating, from tea room snacks and light
lunches at the **El Toreador Coffee Lounge** and the **Alpine**

Coffee Lounge in Horomatangi Street to the extravagantly
expensive and superb **Milly's** (Lane Cover Motel) and **Huka
Lodge** (see below).

Great lake views and excellent New Zealand fare, plus an
odd but tasty assortment of international dishes, makes **Echo
Cliff**, 5 Tongariro Street, tel. 88-539, popular with locals.
Dinner on Friday to Sunday (with reservations) or
smorgasbord lunch at the **Huka Homestead Restaurant**,
tel. 82-245, in the historic village on Huka Falls Road
combines exceptional sightseeing and dining. In town,
Brookes, 22 Tuwharetoa Street, tel. 85-919, offers excellent
value for money with a range of dishes from seafood to steak
dishes.

La Vieille France, 133 Tongariro Street, tel. 84-220,
offers fine French provincial dishes and superb lake views.

Consider treating yourself at the **Huka Lodge**, 85-791, on
the banks of the Waikato, where you'll fantasise about
spending a week rather than merely having dinner.
Conviviality, quiet elegance and exquisitely tasteful decor
combine perfectly with pre-dinner and dinner drinks, food
and wine selections, for less than NZ$100 (£40) per person.
In quite another sphere, the **THC Wairakei Hotel**'s main
restaurant, tel. 48-021, gives you an excellent dinner at about
a quarter the Huka's price. You get what you pay for.

Itinerary options from Rotorua

Mokoia Island in the middle of Lake Rotorua is reached by a
two-hour launch cruise (Rotorua Launch Service, tel.
479-852) for a dip in Hinemoa's hot pool, NZ$18 (£7) adult,
NZ$6 (£2.40) child. Lake Okataina, the most unspoiled of the
lakes surrounding Rotorua, is reached by a scenic drive along
lakes Rotoiti, Rotoehu and Rotomo. The Eastern Walkway
(six-hour round trip) starts at the northern end of the lake at
Tauranganui Bay and finishes four miles later at Humphries
Bay on Lake Tarawera. Hell's Gate, ten miles east of Rotorua
on Highway 30, consists of ten acres of volcanic activity
highlighted by the Kakahi hot waterfall. Orakei Korako, 12
miles off the Rotorua-Taupo Highway, is one of the finest
thermal areas. Board a jet boat to cross Lake Ohakuri, formed
by a hydroelectric dam that submerged three-quarters of the
silica deposits. The remaining terraces coloured by sinter and
algae are well worth seeing. Nearby is Alladins Cave with its
mirror-like pool of jade green water. Flightseeing excursions
(Floatplane Air Services, tel. 84-069) land on a strip on Mt.
Tarawera's summit for a great view of the crater and
surrounding region, NZ$60 (£24) per person.

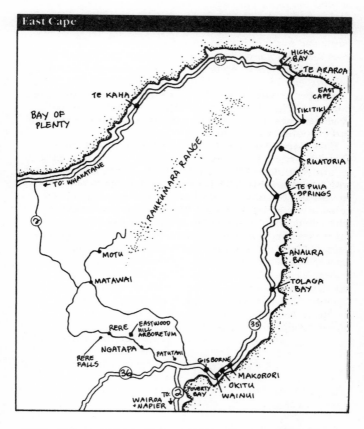

East Cape

Huka Village in Huka Falls Road, a little over a mile from Taupo, is an authentic reconstruction of a New Zealand pioneer village of a hundred years ago. Open daily 10:00 a.m. to 5:00 p.m., NZ$3.50 (£1.40) adult, children free.

If you have plenty of time, there are several intriguing possibilities for further explorations from Rotorua:

Lake Waikaremoana: Follow Highway 38 south of Rotorua to Wairoa on the coastal Highway 2, then on to the unspoiled wilderness of Urewera National Park and the park's gem, Lake Waikaremoana. Driving is most convenient, but a bus from Rotorua to and through the park runs twice a week. On a summer afternoon, take the two-hour Huiarau launch trip

around the lake from Home Bay. Visit the park and you'll
find incredible vegetation and waterfalls—as well as fog, mist,
and chronically wet conditions. The drive takes four to five
hours and much of it is on unsurfaced road. The Wairoa bus
goes there twice a week, on Tuesdays and Thursdays. Stop at
park headquarters at Aniwaniwa for trail information, fishing
permits, etc. In addition to many short walking trails, from
November to March consider a five-day trek from Ruatahuna
down the Whakatane Valley or three to four days on the
Waikaremoana Track, starting at Onepoto, for vast panoramas
and beautiful views of the lake.

East Cape: Another alternative is to head eastward to
Opotiki, circling East Cape to Gisborne, 201 miles (2 days) of
isolated splendour, idyllic golden beaches and picnic spots
with lots of sunshine, camping on deserted sandy bays,
ancient and beautiful pohutukawa trees, rugged mountains
creating major rivers (Waipu, Waipaoa and remote Motu)
with outstanding white-water rafting and canoeing challenges,
superb cycling, and visits to elegantly carved Maori meeting
houses. Along the way there are two beautiful walkways:
Anaura Bay Walkway through the Anaura Scenic Reserve,
and the Cooks Cove Walkway at the end of Tolaga Bay, each
less than six miles there and back. When you finally arrive in
Gisborne, the treat awaiting you is the Bread and Roses
restaurant (tel. 86-697) for excellent crepes, quiches,
vegetarian dishes and fresh bread.

TOUR 9

LAKE TAUPO—TONGARIRO NATIONAL PARK—WANGANUI

Depart very early from Taupo for sightseeing on the slopes of Mt. Ruapehu in Tongariro National Park. From the Park, head for Wanganui, the 'Garden City' on the Tasman Sea, for a relaxing evening.

Suggested schedule

8:00 a.m.	Breakfast and check out.
11:00 a.m.	Explore Taupo and have an early lunch.
1:00 p.m.	Leave Taupo for Turangi.
2:00 p.m.	Arrive in Turangi and visit the Trout Hatchery.
2:30 p.m.	Leave for Ohakune.
4:00 p.m.	Arrive in Ohakune and drive up Ohakune Mountain Rd. on Mt. Ruapehu. See the sunset from Turoa ski lift.
5:30 p.m.	Leave for Wanganui.
8:00 p.m.	Arrive in Wanganui, check in and prepare for dinner.
8:30 p.m.	Dinner and an evening stroll before bed.

Lake Taupo to Wanganui

Take Highway 1 to Turangi. Trout fishing is an option in the Tongariro River. Otherwise, visit the Tongariro Trout Hatchery, a little over a mile south of town on Highway 1. Look carefully for the small sign. From Turangi it is about an hour and a half's drive to Ohakune on Highway 1, turning west onto Highway 49 at Waiouru. This stretch of Highway 1 is called the Desert Road as it passes through Rangipo Desert, an inhospitable area of sand dunes and gravel created by the mountains that force prevailing westerlies to give up their moisture. From Ohakune you can drive straight up Mt. Ruapehu's south-western flank along Ohakune Mountain Road. East of the Desert Road and the parallel Tongariro River you drive past the Kaimanawa State Forest Park, entirely forested with mountain, red and silver beech. Return to Highway 49 west to Raetihi, where you'll turn south along Highway 4 to Wanganui, about 2½ hours without any hurry.

Although travel is better by car, through lake and forest

areas, desert and deep gorges, the main Auckland-Wellington
railway line runs through the western part of the region,
stopping at National Park, Ohakune and Taumarunui, where
jetboats head down the upper Wanganui River to Pipiriki.
Jetboats and buses continue down the Wanganui Valley to
Wanganui. NZR Road Services and Newmans buses serve all
main points in the region and south to Wellington and north
to Auckland. Bonnici Coachlines (tel. 58-456) also runs to
Auckland and Wellington. River City Tracks operates daily
from Ohakune to Wanganui (tel. 58-395).

Sightseeing highlights

● ●**Tongariro Trout Hatchery** tells about the history of
trout fishing in the area. In the underwater viewing chamber
downstairs, you can observe trout of all sizes. In winter you
can watch the spawning process.

● ● ●**Tongariro National Park,** New Zealand's first,
consists of three volcanoes: Tongariro (6,458 feet), Ngauruhoe
(7,515 feet), and Ruapehu (9,175 feet). All three volcanoes
have erupted within memory, showering forest and scrub with
hot ash, most recently Mount Ruapehu in 1975. For
information and interesting displays covering the park's
geology, volcanic activity, flora and fauna, hiking trails and
walking tours, stop at the Tongariro National Park
Headquarters in Whakapapa Village (tel. 729) or the Ohakune
Ranger Station and Park Information Centre at the start of
Ohakune Road (tel. 58-578) from 8:00 a.m. to 5:00 p.m.

●**Ohakune** is the starting point for many rafting, fishing,
hiking and canoeing trips, as well as the winter base for skiers
in the national park and the Kaimanawa State Forest Park.
From Ohakune drive up Ruapehu's south-western flank
traversing the park's various climatic zones.

Where to stay

For NZ$8 (£3.20) a night, you can stay at Wanganui's small
(12 people) **YHA Hostel,** 3 Tregenna Street, tel. 42-804, at
the mouth of the Wanganui River near the beach and on a
city bus line. The **YWCA,** 232 Wicksteed Street, tel. 57-480,
is a comfortable small house in the town centre.

The cabins of the **Alwyn Motor Court,** 65 Karaka Street,
tel. 44-500, and those out at **Castlecliff Beach,** NZ$20 (£8)
doubles, or at the beautifully situated **Aramoho Motor
Camp,** Somme Parade, tel. 38-402, NZ$35 (£14) double,
about four miles outside town, have everything two people (or
more) need. The old-fashioned and charming **Riverside Inn,**
2 Plymouth Street, tel. 32-529, at NZ$33 (£13) double, is a

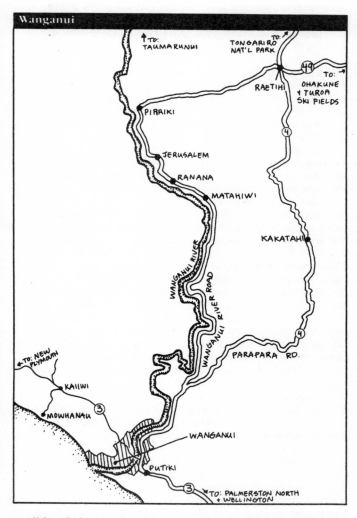

small hotel close to the town centre that is equally good value.

The best quality hotels, serviced motels, motels and motor inns in Wanganui are NZ\$46–\$62 (£18.50–£25) twin/double. Take your pick from more than a dozen with all facilities and amenities, in garden and park-like settings, within minutes of the town centre: **Avro Motel**, 36 Alma Road, tel. 55-279,

with excellent caravan facilities; the **Acacia Park Motel**, 140
Anzac Parade, tel. 39-093, the **Collegiate Motor Inn**, 122
Liverpool Street, tel. 59-309, the **River City Motel**, 30
Somme Parade, tel. 39-107, and others.

Where to eat
For memorable meals in Wanganui, eat along the riverside or
picnic in nearby parks. Plan to have lunch or dinner along the
river at the inexpensive **Riverside Tavern Garden Bistro**,
33 Somme Parade, or the more pricey and less casual
Riverina Restaurant, tel. 38-656.

Other alternatives are to pack a gourmet lunch at **The
Cellers and Deli** for a trip to the beautiful Virginia Park or
wait until you get to the park for lunch at the **Shangri-La
Restaurant** in Great North Road.

In town, **Capers** in Victoria Court may be better looking,
but one of the most pleasant eating experiences is a light
lunch in the Tudor Court Arcade terrace at **Dr. Johnson's
Coffee Lounge** in Victoria Avenue.

Itinerary options
Lake Taupo—Turangi: Try the easy three-hour walk along
the river from Taupo to Aratiatia or vice versa. Turangi, at
the southern end of Lake Taupo on the banks of the
Tongariro River, is the self-proclaimed 'Heart of the Great
New Zealand Outdoors' and 'Trout Fishing Capital of the
World'. There you can be outfitted, licensed, and pumped full
of valuable information to fish in the best places for brown
trout in March-April and rainbow trout in May-September.
Local fishing guides are available.

Rafting enthusiasts, contact **Turangi White Water
Rafting** (tel. Turangi 8856) for white-water thrills on the
Tongariro or Mohaka Rivers or wilderness fishing trips.
There are bus services to Turangi from all major and
secondary cities.

Tongariro National Park: For ramblers, the Ketetahi
Track from Highway 47 near Lake Rotoaira to the
Mangatepopo trail hut offers great views over hundreds of
square miles to the north, including all of Lake Taupo. As an
alternative to this two- to three-day hike, Venture Treks, a
local guide service, offers a five-day guided trek, the Mount
Ruapehu Alpine Walk, around the mountain to Ruapehu's
crater lake. In summer, a walk from Whakapapa Village to the
summit of Mt. Tongariro offers breathtaking views across
Tongariro National Park to Lake Taupo, the Kaimanawas and
Mt. Egmont. In winter, Whakapapa is an enormous ski area,

mostly for intermediate and advanced skiers with an uphill capacity of 13,500 skiers an hour. Combine excellent spring skiing with incredible trout fishing or local white-water rafting in the Tongariro or Rangitikei Rivers. National Park Headquarters in Whakapapa will supply all the information, maps, hunting licences and suggested guide services you need. Just 11 miles from Ohakune and an hour's drive from Whakapapa on the southern slopes of Mt. Ruapehu, the Turoa ski area offers plenty of slopes for all levels of skiers.

If you decide to stay over in the Tongariro National Park, here are the range of choices: Ohakune's **YHA Hostel** (tel. 58-724) is next to the Turoa Information Centre. The **Whakapapa Motor Camp** (tel. Ruapehu 897) has the largest variety of accommodation: tent sites, caravan sites, nice cabins (only NZ$24 (£9.50) for a four-berth), and a lodge with bunks.

Rates for hotels, better self-contained ski chalets and lodges with private facilities have zoomed upwards in the last few years but still offer good value when compared to accommodation in European ski areas. Rates are about 30% lower in summer. The **Ruapehu Skotel** (tel. Ruapehu 619) is NZ$90–$100 (£36–£40) double in ski season. Consider spending a night at the elegant and internationally renowned **THC Chateau Tongariro** (tel. Ruapehu 809) as one of your legitimate budget breakers for the trip (NZ$125 (£50)). The Chateau is right in the centre of all skiing and touring activities in an area where accommodation is very limited.

Turangi is an ideal touring base for both National Park and Taupo-Tongariro area activities, with a wide variety of accommodation, camping and caravan parks. Campers should consider heading for the **Mahuia Campground** about three miles from the National Park on Highway 47, one of the best in New Zealand—and free.

The Wanganui River Road is an alternative to heading south on Highway 4 from Raetihi to Wanganui. Adjacent to the river are good trails to waterfalls, the remains of Maori villages, scenic viewpoints in the hills above the river, and Jerusalem, one of the most photogenic villages on the North Island, nestling on a green carpet in a bush-rimmed riverbend, red roofs on white walls surrounding a delicate church spire. Above Pipiriki, to Taumarunui, the river and its 239 rapids are navigable only by jetboats or canoes. Contact **Pipiriki Jet Boat Tours** (tel. Raetihi 54633) for information.

TOUR 10

WANGANUI-WELLINGTON

Take a relaxing break from driving. Stroll in Wanganui's lovely parks, travel by riverboat up the tranquil Wanganui for a wine-tasting tour, and visit a regional museum before driving down the scenic west ('Kapiti') coast to Wellington on very good roads.

Suggested schedule

8:30 a.m.	Breakfast.
9:30 a.m.	Durie Hill vistas.
10:30 a.m.	Visit your choice of parks or museum.
12:30 p.m.	Lunch and check out.
2:00 p.m.	Tour the Holly Lodge Estate Winery along the Wanganui River.
4:30 p.m.	Return to Wanganui and depart for Wellington.
6:30 p.m.	Break for dinner near Levin on the west coast.
9:00 p.m.	Arrive in Wellington and check in.

Transport

Highway 1 to Wellington, the most direct route down the Kapiti Coast, has pretty pastoral scenes followed by good beach stops and outstanding sea views. The region around Levin is a major fruit and vegetable producing area. In season, pick up your lunch at roadside stalls. Starting at Levin, Highway 1 runs between the coast and the Tararua Range, with forest-covered 2000- to 3000-foot mountains.

Heading south from Levin is a long stretch of golden sand beaches—Waikanae, Paraparaumu and Raumati—in Wellington's suburbs. Avid shell collectors, bring large bags to Paekakariki. South of Paekakariki take the winding Paekakariki Hill Road for good views of Porirua Harbour to the south-west.

Sightseeing highlights

● ●**Wanganui**'s tree-lined riverfront, green hills and many lovely parks make it one of New Zealand's more picturesque cities. Visit the 'Garden City's' Cook's Gardens, Queen's Park, the Aramoho Park, Moutoa Gardens, Victoria Park, Peat Park, and especially beautiful Virginia Lake. Also see

Bushy Park, 15 miles north-west of Wanganui, a fine old
home with spacious gardens and a bush park, open
Wednesday to Sunday, 10:00 a.m. to 5:00 p.m. Call in at the
Hospitality Wanganui Information Centre on Guyton Street
for maps, brochures and even a personalised tour guide (free).
● ●**The Wanganui River** offers a pleasant riverboat (or
jetboat) journey up the lower river. For information on the
historic *MV Waireka* riverboat trip to Hipango Park with a
stop at the Holly Lodge Estate, tel. 36-346. NZ$17 (£6.80)
adult, NZ$8.50 (£3.40) child. For information on jetboats
contact Wanganui River Jet Tours, tel. 36-346.
● ●**Wanaganui Regional Museum** in Queen's Park, one of
the best in the country, houses a large and exceptional Maori
collection, including a 75-foot war canoe. Open weekdays
from 9:30 a.m. to 4:30 p.m., weekends 1:00 to 4:30 p.m.
● ●**Durie Hill** (216 feet) at the south end of the Wanganui
Bridge provides a splendid view of the region. Take the lift to
a platform at the summit. For an even better view, if you're
energetic, ascend the Durie Hill War Memorial Tower.

Where to stay

The Ivanhoe Inn, 52 Ellice Street, tel. 842-264, on the
Mount Victoria hillside, has spacious singles, twins and
double rooms to offer hostellers at NZ$10–$24 (£4–£9.50).
Also on Mount Victoria, **Beethoven House**, 89 Brougham
Street, tel. 842-226, is a non-YHA 'B&B hostel' for
non-smokers who love (or can tolerate) continuous Beethoven,
and can afford NZ$11 (£4.40). In the centre of town,
convenient to all transport and attractions, the **YHA Hostel**,
40 Tinakori Road, tel. 736-271, is NZ$11 (£4.40). Campers
should plan to find sites outside of Wellington such as the
Hutt Park Motor Camp, 95 Hutt Park Road, tel. 685-913,
at NZ$6 (£2.40) for two. As an alternative, try the **YHA
Hostel**, no phone, in the hill country of Kaitoke at the top of
the Hutt Valley.

There is no YMCA or YWCA, but the 170-room **Railton
Travel Hotel**, 213 Cuba Street, tel. 851-632, a B&B with the
option of three meals, is the next best thing. The double rate
of NZ$45 (£18) is a bargain. The 60-room **Rowena Budget
Travel Hotel**, 115 Brougham Street, tel. 857-872, is
comparably good B&B value. For hilltop views of the city and
harbour, plenty of exercise for those without cars, thick with
character and comfort, try the **Fairview Lodge**, 8 Church
Street, tel. 726-248, a B&B at NZ$40 (£16) double.

Look for inexpensive accommodation (NZ$48 (£19) for a
twin/double) outside Wellington, such as the **Spinnaker**

Motel, tel. 33-8171, in Plimmerton or the **Safari Park
Motel**, tel. 36-054, in Waikanae. In a year, in-town 'budget'
motel flat rates have gone up from NZ$54 (£21.50) to NZ$65
(£26) for central, fully equipped and attractive units, such as
those of **The Apollo Lodge**, 49 Majoribanks Street, tel.
851-849, the **Majoribanks Apartments**, 38 Majoribanks
Street, tel. 857-305, and the **Wellington Luxury Motel**, 14
Hobson Street, tel. 726-825.

Among central hotels with superior or luxury standards,
which means over NZ$110 (£44) for a twin/double, the very
attractive and central **West Plaza**, 110 Wakefield Street, tel.
731-440, stands out for two or three people at NZ$90 (£36).
An extravagance on the Terrace above the business district,
the **James Cook Hotel** on The Terrace, tel. 725-865, at
NZ$125–$150 (£50–£60) single, twin or double, literally
stands above the rest. As a bonus, lifts go down to the city as
well as up to the rooms.

Where to eat

For the best combination of views of harbour and city, food,
service and atmosphere, take the Kelburn cable car to the
Skyline, 1 Upland Road, Kelburn, tel. 758-727. Or, if the
cable car ride, fresh air and twinkling stars go to your head,
you can try to get a table at **Marbles**, Kelburn Villas, tel.
758-490, or **Le Routier**, 92 Upland Road, tel. 758-981.

Otherwise, you'll find good-to-excellent restaurants and
cafes all over Wellington. For a plentiful salad bar, try
Suzie's Coffee Bar and Restaurant at 108 Willis Street, or
soup and salads at **The Great New Zealand Soup Kitchen**,
32 Waring Taylor Street near Lambton Quay. For natural
foods, an excellent choice is **That's Natural**, 88 Manners
Street, tel. 736-681; or **Amrita Vegetarian Restaurant**,
127 Cuba Mall.

Before leaving the North Island, try the great charcoaled
steaks at **Beefeater**, 105 The Terrace, tel. 738-195. **Il
Casino**, 108 Tory Street, tel. 857-496, is the best North
Italian restaurant in New Zealand for decor and fine pasta,
seafood, gnocchi and other tasty dishes. The French
restaurant with the best views of the harbour is **Grain of
Salt**, 232 Oriental Parade, tel. 848-642. If you prefer really
good hamburgers and sundaes, stop down the street at
Rockefellers, 132 Oriental Parade, tel. 846-975.

Around Country Place, restaurants seem to progress
alphabetically up the street: rarified atmosphere and prices at
the **Bacchus**, 8 Courtney Place, tel. 846-592, where you can
order anything confidently; BYO French lunch or dinner at

Chez Nigel, 29A Courtney Place, tel. 844-535; **Java**, 99
Courtney Place, tel. 857-620, for one of the most interesting
dining experiences in Wellington; and delicious venison dishes
at **Marcel's**, 104 Courtney Place, tel. 842-159.

Itinerary options

Consider a wine trip via paddle-steamer (tel. 39-344) to the
Holly Lodge Estate Winery. The *Otonui* has been on the river
for 80 years. The 2½-hour trip departs Monday to Friday at
10:00 a.m., weekends 10:00 a.m. and 2:00 p.m., NZ$11
(£4.40) adult, NZ$5 (£2) child. From the winery, take the
jetboat trip to Hipango Park. Holly Lodge operates these
jetboat tours, which leave at 10:00 a.m. and 2:00 p.m. for the
12-mile trip to Hipango Park Scenic Reserve (two hours there
and back).

For a special adventure, try a jetboat trip up the most
scenic and exciting stretch of the Wanganui River north of
Pipiriki. Choose the most interesting places on the river from
a local map (see the PRO) and select the corresponding
jetboat tour, from 35-minute local tours to trips to Hipango
Park (12 miles), Manapurua, Drap Scene, costing about
NZ$22–$50 (£9–£20) for adults.

John Hammond's River Road Tours offers a complete
river tour by minibus with a stop in the picturesque Maori
village of Jerusalem.

TOUR 11

WELLINGTON

Enjoy leisurely sightseeing on Marine Drive, overlooking the
harbour from many different viewpoints, followed by a cable
car ride for dinner and views of the city from the Kelburn
Terminal area. In between, tour the city's most interesting
architectural, historical and cultural attractions. All the while,
enjoy no fog, no smog, and no pollution in 'Windy
Wellington'.

Suggested schedule

8:30 a.m.	Breakfast.
9:30 a.m.	Depart for Marine Drive.
12:00 noon	Picnic lunch along Marine Drive.
1:30 p.m.	Drop off your car, then tour Parliament buildings.
2:30 p.m.	National Museum and Art Gallery.
4:00 p.m.	Cable car to Kelburn and the Botanic Gardens.
6:00 p.m.	Dinner and evening at the Top of Victoria.

Transport

The Wellington City Corporation bus system mainly operates
south of the city. Trains are used to the north. Eastern,
western and southern bus routes start at the railway station on
Waterloo Quay or at Courtney Place. Pick up timetables from
news-stands. Four commuter trains run to Upper and Lower
Hutt and other northern destinations. NZRR buses run up
the peninsula's west coast and centre (tel. 725-399 for bus and
rail information). Newmans Coach Tours operate east coast
intercity services. Mount Cook Landlines runs between
Wellington and Auckland (11 hours). Day (Silver Fern) and
night (Northerner) trains to Auckland and intermediate points
leave Monday to Saturday from the New Zealand Railways
Terminal.

Orientation

Approach Wellington along the 'Gold Coast', actually an
elongated suburb on the western edge of the southern
peninsula. The rugged mountain forests of the Rimutakas and
Tararua Ranges separate the Wairapa Plain to the east from
the western coastal area.

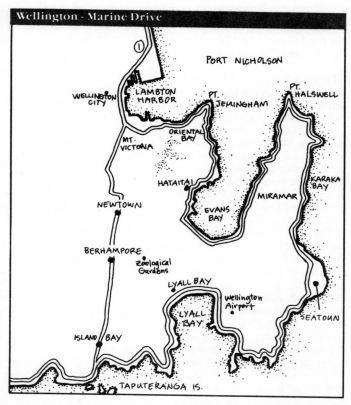

Wellington - Marine Drive

New Zealand's capital city at the tip of this peninsula is set in a green amphitheatre on a sparkling harbour. On a sunny and windy day, Wellington becomes a very beautiful city. Wellington can be best appreciated from the Cook Strait ferry heading through the harbour, from the top of Mount Victoria or at various points on the 24-mile Marine Drive, especially from the north side of Miramar Peninsula. The winds funnelling through Wellington from Cook Strait produce crisp, clear views of the surrounding forested peninsulas, the pastel wooden buildings climbing the hills above Oriental Bay, and the conglomeration of government and office buildings rimming the waterfront.

At weekends the government and business population disappears and, unlike Auckland, it's a good time to visit and bargain for reduced hotel rates. Otherwise book in advance.

Good city bus services from the railway station will take care
of your transport needs. For bookings and other information,
use the Information Office at the railway centre or the
Government Tourist Bureau.

Sightseeing highlights

●●**Marine Drive** hugs the harbour shore for 24 miles,
skirting Oriental and Evans Bays, looping around Miramar
Peninsula, where there are fine views of the harbour at the
Massey Memorial. Several soft sandy swimming beaches,
including Scorching, Karaka and Worser Bays in the inner
harbour and Lyall and Island Bays in the outer harbour, offer
inviting places to stop and see spectacular bush-covered hills
around the bright blue bay waters.

●The circular domed **Parliament**, the 'Beehive', houses the
government's executive offices. Free tours are conducted
hourly from 9:00 a.m. to 3:30 p.m.

●**The Old Government Building** at the northern end of
Lambton Quay is one of the largest all-wooden buildings in
the world. In a city where old edifices are rapidly being
replaced by modern office structures, this wooden Italianate
civic building is all the more rare and precious.

●●**The National Museum** has an excellent Maori and
Pacific Island collection (11:00 a.m. to 4:45 p.m. daily). Also
see the adjoining National Art Gallery, with New Zealand and
international art.

●**City Council's 2½-hour afternoon bus tour,** costing
NZ$8 (£3.20), is an inexpensive and easy way to see all of
Wellington's sightseeing highlights.

●●●**Cable cars** climb for about four minutes up to the
Kelburn terminal from Cable Car Lane off Lambton Quay in
the heart of the shopping district. The cost is NZ$.55 (£0.22)
adult, NZ$.25 (£0.10) child, single. From there, walk down
through the Botanic Gardens and the Lady Norwood Rose
Gardens, through Thorndon, where some of the city's older
wooden cottages (dating from the 1870s) cluster on Ascot
Street.

TOUR 12

WELLINGTON TO CHRISTCHURCH

Over a thousand years ago the original Polynesian settlers in
the Marlborough Sounds region started hunting moa, the
giant flightless relative of the ostrich, until inevitable
extinction. Four hundred Maoris watched in astonishment as
Capt. James Cook's *HMS Endeavour* sailed past in 1770. Abel
Tasman had been the first European arrival, 128 years before
the *Endeavour* dropped anchor, but Tasman stayed only a few
days before sailing north. After claiming the land for the King
and naming the sound after Queen Charlotte, Cook
circumnavigated the South Island, returned to the Sound to
reprovision, and sailed back to England, revisiting the Sound
four more times for a total of 15 weeks between 1770 and
1777. The bush-covered hillsides of Queen Charlotte Sound
that you pass aboard the Inter-Island Ferry from Wellington
to Picton were heavily forested in Cook's time. Today you'll
still have no difficulty understanding why it was one of his
favourite anchorages.

As in the Bay of Islands, closer to the equator but actually
less sunny and warm, you can charter yachts and cruisers, hire
fishing boats of all kinds and find a remote island, bay or cove
with white sand beaches for a get-away day or week, or join a
variety of cruises almost any time of day. There's over 600
miles of coastline to choose from. Behind the Sounds are
warm hills and valleys with fruit orchards and vineyards,
national parks with trout-filled lakes and rivers, and even
mountains for skiing.

Suggested schedule

7:00 a.m.	Breakfast and check out.
9:00 a.m.	Inter-Island Ferry across Cook Strait to Picton. Lunch on board.
2:00 p.m.	Train or bus to Christchurch.
8:00 p.m.	Arrive Christchurch and check in.
9:00 p.m.	Late dinner and evening stroll along the Avon.

Transport

I recommend that you return your hired car in Wellington
(without penalty or one-way charge) and pick up another
car in Christchurch from the same hire company,

continuing your weekly agreement.

Between Wellington and Picton on the South Island there are four ferry services daily each way. For NZ$16.70 (£6.70) (cars from NZ$70 (£28) depending on size), the crossing in daylight and with good weather is a scenic, enjoyable trip.

The train, which is more quaint than comfortable, leaves the Picton station near the ferry landing at 2:10 p.m. and arrives in Christchurch at 8:05 p.m. The cost, NZ$20.60 (£8.25) is a little more than Newman's bus service, which also meets the ferry and gets to Christchurch a bit faster. Take your choice: more comfort on the bus, a more unusual travel experience on the train.

If you decide to drive, book ferry space for the car or camper van as far in advance as possible (months ahead, for travel during New Zealand holidays). The wharf terminal buildings at Wellington are off Aotea Quay. The turn-off is clearly marked by road signs. Report one hour before sailing time. Driver and passengers must have passenger tickets.

From Picton, train and bus travellers as well as drivers will follow Highway 1 south through Blenheim, along the Seaward Kaikoura range and its narrow, wild indented coastline. In Kaikoura, motorists can take a break in the six-hour trip to walk along the shoreline and have refreshments.

Sightseeing highlight
● ● ●**Marlborough Sounds Maritime Park** region contains a marvellous variety of outdoor recreation. From Picton, Havelock and Motueka, hire charter yachts, line-fishing boats, and game-fishing boats, cruise to sandy bays, coves, islands and their virtually untouched beaches in the region's deep inlets. The ranger's offices in Blenheim and Havelock, as well as local Visitors' Information Offices, have all the necessary maps, guides and other information.

Where to stay
Christchurch has an abundance of good and reasonably priced accommodation on public transport routes.

There are two hostels in Christchurch: the **Cora Wilding Youth Hostel**, 9 Evelyn Couzins Avenue, tel. 899-199, in a charming old mansion 15 minutes' walk from Cathedral Square; and **Rolleston House**, 5 Worcester Street, tel. 66-564, ten minutes closer to the centre. Both charge NZ$10 (£4).

Within three to six miles from the Square, first-rate caravan sites are available for NZ$11 (£4.40) for two people, some with cabins or tourist flats from NZ$25 to NZ$36

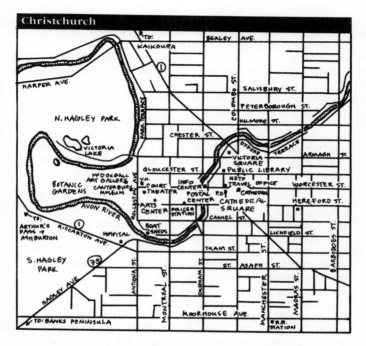

(£10–£14.50): **Amber Park**, 308 Blenheim Road, tel.
483-327; **Meadow Park Motor Camp**, 39 Meadow Street,
tel. 529-176; and **Russley Park Motor Camp**, 372
Yaldhurst Road, tel. 427- 021.

Many excellent guest houses charge NZ$45–$50 (£18–£20)
double or NZ$25 (£10) single, and there are a few real B&B
bargains. Just one block from the square, comfort, simplicity
and reasonable price (NZ$23–$28 (£9–£11) double or twin)
make the **Hereford Private Hotel**, 36 Hereford Street, tel.
799-536, a winning choice. The love and attention lavished on
the interior furnishing and decorations of the **Eliza's Manor
House**, 82 Bealey Avenue, tel. 68-584, a historic trust
mansion, makes this B&B a bargain at NZ$25 (£10) per
person. The cosy **Aaragi Guest House**, 15 Riccarton Road,
tel. 483-584, NZ$42 (£17) double and twin, is further out but
has public transport at the door. With 37 nicely decorated
rooms at NZ$25 (£10) per person, the very popular **Windsor
Private Hotel B&B**, 52 Armagh Street, tel. 61-503, offers
better odds than the other guest houses for room availability.

The **Warners Hotel**, tel. 65-159, an old B&B landmark in the Square, charges NZ$23 (£9) per person. From guest kitchen, to rooms and garden, everything is comfortable about the **Wolseley Lodge**, 107 Papanui Road, tel. 556-202 including the price: NZ$23 (£9) per person. The **Hotel Melville**, 49 Gloucester Street, tel. 798-956, at NZ$19 (£7.50) is also worth investigating.

There are countless very good motels in Christchurch at NZ$45 (£18) and up. NZ$55 (£22) for two people gives you a choice of five-star motels. 'Bargains' in good motels, both close in and further out, cost NZ$31–$39 (£12.50–£15.50): the **City Court**, 850 Colombo Street, tel. 69-099; **Fairlane Court Motel**, 69 Linwood Avenue, tel. 894-943; **Holiday Lodge Motel**, 862 Colombo Street, tel. 66-584; and **Salisbury Motel**, 206 Salisbury Street, tel. 68-713.

Where to eat

An ample variety of cafés and tearooms is distributed around Christchurch to take care of breakfast and lunch needs, but a visit to the Garden City merits something a bit more special. Smorgasbord fans shouldn't miss **The Gardens Restaurant and Tea Kiosk**, tel. 65-076, in the Botanic Gardens. French provincial fare at the **Restaurante Sorbonne**, tel. 50-566, or a bowl of soup and veg at the **Dux de Lux Gourmet Vegetarian Restaurant**, tel. 66-919, both sharing the atmosphere of the Christchurch Arts Centre on Montreal Street, make excellent choices for lunch. Also, enjoy smoked salmon at **Grimsby's**, Montreal Street, tel. 799-040, a wonderful old building, or a fish and salad lunch, with delicious desserts, at the **Greenhouse Restaurant**, 663A Colombo Street, tel. 68-524.

You won't be overwhelmed by the outstanding choices for dinner in Christchurch. Two places that could easily qualify are the **Sign of the Takahe**, tel. 324-052, in a wonderful stone building with great views of the Lyttelton Harbour Estuary and Christchurch from the Cashmere Hills, excellent international cuisine and service, and the waterfront location and excellent French-style food at BYO **Scarborough Fare** in Sumner, seven miles south-east of Christchurch, tel. 27-6987.

Other recommended dining alternatives include: **Leinster**, 158 Leinster Road, Merivale, tel. 588-866; **Michael's**, 178 High Street, tel. 60-822; steak at the **Forget-Me-Not**, 12 Wakefield Street, Sumner, tel. 26-6501, about seven miles south-east of Christchurch; and the *prix fixe* French menu at **Portstone**, 471 Ferry Road, tel. 896-529. Extra large appetites will be well rewarded by a visit to the **Wagon Wheel Restaurant**, Papanui Road, tel. 556-159, for steak, chicken, seafood and excellent desserts. If you want salad along with the same basics, try the **Jail Restaurant**, 106 Gloucester Street, tel. 66-553.

Itinerary options

If you have plenty of time, instead of heading directly to Christchurch, tour the Marlborough Sounds region. Visit Nelson's Botanic Gardens, Matai Valley and Tahuna Beach. Thirty-five miles to the north-west is Kaiteriteri, the best beach in the area. (Watch out for the katipo, a poisonous spider that lurks in beach driftwood.) See the view of Tasman Bay from Takaka Hill. The Nelson area's high-quality pottery clays have contributed to a thriving pottery craft in Nelson, Hope, Brightwater and Wakefield. Lots of ceramics, glasswork, weaving, jewellery, woodcraft, and other arts and crafts are also found in the Nelson area.

Sail in the beautiful Kenepuru Sound off Pelorus Sound. Pelorus is the most extensive sound (32 miles) with the finest scenery. Fish for cod, terakiki, snapper, garfish, grouper and kahawai. Surfcast between Kaikoura and Cape Koamaru. Flyfish in the Rai, Pelorus, Wairau and Opawa Rivers and Spring Creek for brown trout. In summer, try salmon fishing in the Wairau River.

Visit vineyards in Redwoods Valley, Ruby Bay, Upper Moutere and especially Blenheim's Wairau Valley. Ski in Rainbow Valley, west of Blenheim and enjoy outstanding views. Flightsee over the region from Nelson, Blenheim and Motueka.

From Nelson go west on Highway 60 toward Motueka and Abel Tasman National Park with its golden beaches, rocky headlands and tidal inlets. Enter the Park at Marohau. To return, hire a taxi from Motueka to pick you up in Totaranui, at the north end of the park, or charter a boat in Motueka or Kaiteriteri. A simpler alternative might be Abel Tasman National Park Enterprises' four-day launch trip and guided walk, which includes three nights at The Lodge at Torrent Bay.

In the North-West Nelson State Forest (930,000 acres) is one of New Zealand's best-known tracks, the Heaphy Track, a 42-mile (one-way), five-day hike linking Golden Bay at the Abel Tasman National Park with the west coast. There are seven huts and five shelters, but they can be crowded at any time of year so pack your own tent.

TOUR 13

CHRISTCHURCH REGION

Stroll along the Avon, people-watch in Cathedral Square, visit
the museums and Arts Centre, see Gothic and Victorian
architecture, and experience the tranquillity of Christchurch.
Leave Christchurch in the afternoon over the Port Hills to
Lyttleton, then return to the urbane delights of the city's
centre.

Suggested schedule

8:00 a.m.	Leisurely breakfast.
9:00 a.m.	Stroll along the Avon and walking tour around city centre.
12:00 noon	Picnic lunch on the banks of the Avon.
1:00 p.m.	Port Hills drive.
6:30 p.m.	Dinner.
8:30 p.m.	Attend theatre at the Arts Centre.

Orientation

Christchurch was planned by a young English Tory, John
Robert Godley, to be an English city, and the magnificent
parks and gardens adjoining the serpentine Avon River attest
to that vision. In contrast to other New Zealand cities,
Christchurch's centre is a pleasure for pedestrians. It is a
place to be seen on bicycle, foot and boat.

There are fine examples of colonial wooden architecture
such as the homes along Bealey Avenue and the McLeans
Mansion in Manchester Street; distinguished commercial
buildings include the Pegasus Press building in Oxford
Terrace and the Occidental Hotel in Hereford.

The city's urban amenities balance its regional outdoor
recreation and scenic highlights: the inner city with the
beautiful Avon, Hagley Park and Botanic Gardens, and
Cathedral Square, and the city's perimeter with Summit Road
atop Port Hills, the very special Banks Peninsula, and
picturesque Canterbury farms. Further afield are the Rakaia,
Rangitata, and Waimakariri Rivers and lakes for fishing or
rafting, snow-clad Mt. Hutt, thermal Hamner Springs' hills
and exotic forests and the spectacular Arthur's Pass National
Park. The Canterbury Information Centre (75 Worcester
Street, at the corner of Oxford Terrace, tel. 799-629) and the

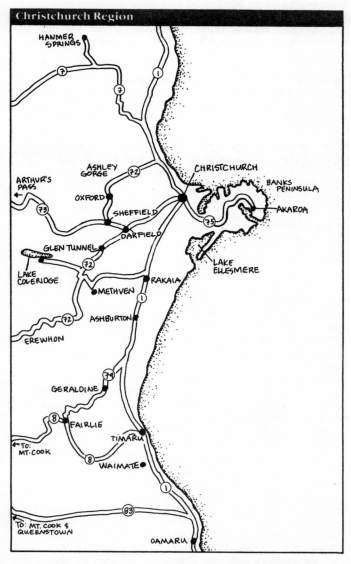

Christchurch Region

NZTP Travel Office (Government Life Building, Cathedral Square, tel. 794-900) will take care of most of your needs for

information, maps, brochures, bookings, tickets for local
attractions, vehicle hire and tours. For complete information
and advice on outdoor activities and tour operators in the
Christchurch region, visit the Outdoor Recreation Centre in
the Arts Centre (tel. 799-395).

Inner Canterbury walking tour

Cathedral Square is the centre of the city. Colombo Street
runs north and south through it. From the entrance to the
cathedral, Worcester Street leads west toward Hagley Park.
Christchurch Cathedral (Anglican), the finest Gothic style
church in New Zealand, soars almost 200 feet. Climb the 133
narrow stone steps through the bell chamber to the balconies
of the tower 100 feet above the Square where you get a great
view of the city, plains and even the Southern Alps on a clear
day.

From the Square, walk north along Colombo Street to
Victoria Square, turn though the Square to Victoria Street
and the **Avon River**. Gracefully winding its way through the
city, the grassy banks dotted with flowerbeds, weeping
willows and old oaks, daffodils in spring and ornate bridges is
the main feature of Christchurch's 'English' character and
charm. Bicycles and canoes are the best ways to tour the Avon
and the historic and modern buildings lining the river.

Cross the Avon to the **floral clock artwork** in Victoria
Street at the corner of Chestnut Street on the way to the
Town Hall in Kilmore Street. In a city of history and fine
old buildings, this very modern glass-and-marble structure is
a bold contrast. You can stroll through the building on
weekdays between 9:00 a.m. and 5:00 p.m. or take a guided
tour between 11:00 a.m. and 3:00 p.m. for NZ\$1.50 (£0.60)
adult, NZ\$.75 (£0.30) child. Outside is the beautiful **Ferrier
Fountain**. Continue along the Avon to the Gothic
Provincial Government Buildings on the corner of
Durham and Armagh Streets, built between 1859 and 1865,
the only remaining provincial government buildings in New
Zealand (the system was abolished in 1876). The Stone
Chamber is open daily from 9:00 a.m. to 4:00 p.m.

At Worcester Street turn left (west) to the **Arts Centre of
Christchurch**. Housed in the neo-Gothic former University
of Canterbury, the centre is now the home for day and
evening performing and visual arts, craft, dramatic,
instrumental and choral groups, shopping and restaurants. If
you're strolling on Saturday during the summer, an Arts,
Crafts and Antique Market is held in the centre from 10:00
a.m. to 3:00 p.m. The Arts Centre Information Office in the

clock tower is open for information and bookings daily from
8:30 a.m. to 5:00 p.m. (tel. 60-988).

Across Rolleston Avenue, at the entrance to the Botanic
Gardens and adjacent to the **McDougall Art Gallery**, the
region's major art museum, is the **Canterbury Museum**.
The museum contains outstanding displays of early Maori
culture during the moa hunting era, mounted birds, Oriental
art, a reconstruction of colonial Christchurch, and the Hall of
Antarctic Discovery. Open daily from 10:00 a.m. to 4:30 p.m.
Behind the museum, bounded by a loop of the Avon, is the
Botanic Gardens, full of native New Zealand plants,
tropical, flowering, alpine and desert plants, orchids, flowering
trees and much more. You may decide to return after lunch
and spend more time in both the museum and the gardens.

Sightseeing highlights
● ● ●**The Avon River** and its grassy tree-shaded banks
winding around Christchurch's inner city provides a superb
pathway, on foot, bicycle or water, to visit the primary
attractions between Hagley Park/Botanic Gardens and Victoria
Square/Town Hall. Hire a canoe from Antigua Boatsheds and
follow the tree-lined Avon downstream past riverside parks,
the Chamber of Commerce Building, Victoria Bridge, the
Christchurch Town Hall and nearby floral clock in Victoria
Square, passing under many picturesque bridges, notably the
Bridge of Remembrance. Enjoy a two-hour riverside walk if
you have the time.
● ●**Cathedral Square** is surrounded by gift and souvenir
shops. North of the square, New Regent Street, Colombo
Street and a network of arcades are full of boutiques and
speciality and antique shops. See the Christchurch Cathedral
tower's panoramic view of the city (9:00 a.m. to 4:00 p.m.
weekdays and Saturday, 12:30 to 4:30 p.m. on Sunday). Red
buses from Cathedral Square leave at 1:30 p.m. for a city and
suburb tour.
● ●**The Town Hall** is New Zealand's most striking modern
town hall design.
●**The Ferrier Fountain** outside the Christchurch Town
Hall and the **Bowler Fountain** in Victoria Square both light
up at night with varied patterns of water and colour.
● ●**The Art Centre Museum and Art Gallery**, formerly
the University, is a focal point for local artists, musicians,
craftspeople, and all types of performers, on stage and in
many shops, with an open air market on Saturdays in the
summer. Check the current calendar for theatre, ballet and
other dance, recitals and arts and crafts exhibits.

● ●**The Nga-Hua-E-Wha National Marae**, comprised of
a meeting house, arts and crafts centre, and the Riki-Rangi
Carving Centre in the Arts Centre, is a showcase of local and
New Zealand Maori culture.
● ●**The Canterbury Museum**, directly across from the
Arts Centre, has the finest Antarctic collection in the world as
well as fine colonial and Maori sections. Open 10:00 a.m. to
4:30 p.m. weekdays, 2:00 to 4:30 p.m. Sunday.
● ●**The Botanic Gardens**—75 acres include spectacular
displays of exotic and native plants and trees. Open 8:00 a.m.
to dusk.
●**The City Mall Complex** contains the Shades Shopping
Precinct, Cashfields and the National Mutual Arcade. It is
linked by an overhead pedestrian walkway to the Canterbury
Centre and the Triangle Centre.
    Fine old gothic-style buildings, dating from the 1870s, dot
the city centre: the Canterbury Provincial Government
Buildings, the Arts Centre, Canterbury Museum, and the
State Trinity Centre; and neo-Gothic or High Victorian
church design in wood and stone: Cathedral Church of Christ,
St. Michael's, All Angels Church, and Cathedral of the
Blessed Sacrament.
● ●**Hagley Park**, a 450-acre haven close to the city centre in
spring has thousands of daffodils blooming in Daffodil
Woodland, and azaleas and rhododendrons in Milbrook
Reserve off North Hagley Park.
●**Port Hills** on Christchurch's outskirts has walkways with
spectacular vistas: Sign of the Takahe, Crater Rim, Mount
Vernon, Sign of the Kiwi, Victoria Park, Nicholson Park,
Scarborough, Godley Head, the Bridle Path, Rapaki Track,
Kennedy's Bush Track, Major Hornbrook's Track and the
Bowenvale Walkway. To reach these walkways, make for
Summit Road on top of the Port Hills, an outstanding drive
or bus tour to Lyttelton Harbour. From heights of over 1,800
feet, the Northern Summit Road has views of Christchurch,
the Seaward Kaikouras to the north, the Southern Alps, and
the Canterbury Plains, and views of many reserves, viewpoints
and walkways.
●**Ferrymead Historic Park**, a 100-acre site next to the
Heathcote River, includes train and tram rides through
vintage township and museum areas displaying the history of
aeronautics, musical instruments, printing, motor- and
horse-drawn vehicles, fire-fighting, military and photographic
equipment, urban transport and railways. Open 10:00 a.m. to
4:30 p.m. daily.
    Christchurch has a wealth of other transport museums: the

Yaldhurst Transport Museum with horse-drawn vehicles, vintage cars, racing cars, steam engines and traction engines; the **Steam Museum** at McLeans Island; and the **Royal New Zealand Air Force Museum**, with 18 aircraft dating from 1910 to the 1970s.

Itinerary options

The Northern and Southern Summit Roads, both of which circle Governor's Bay, return to the city over Gebbie's Pass. Each route is about 60 miles long or 120 miles all told. For the Northern Summit Road, from Hereford Street adjoining Cathedral Square take High Street south-east, which becomes Ferry Road when it crosses Highway 1 (Madras Street). Head toward Lyttelton through Sumner, turning south (right) onto Summit Road. For the Southern Summit Road take Colombo Street but turn right on Summit Road. At Gebbie's Pass Road turn right to Highway 75. To the right, Highway 75 leads back to the city; to the left, out to Banks Peninsula and Akaroa (see Tour 22). The Christchurch Transport Board (tel. 794-600) has a three-hour Port Hills and Harbour Tour with a Lyttelton Harbour launch cruise (NZ$12 (£4.80) adult, NZ$8 (£3.20) child). NZRR Services offers a day-long trip covering both Northern and Southern Summit Roads for NZ$17 (£6.80) per person (tel. 799-020). Try walking the Bridle Path to Lyttelton Harbour (2 hours), or the Godley Head Walkway across Summit Road (2 hours).

Lyttelton, the South Island's leading port, located on the flanks of a flooded volcanic crater, has a fine collection of 19th century buildings and churches. Regular launches shuttle to the attractive Diamond Harbour on the south side of the harbour (tel. Lyttelton 28-8368).

Waimakariri River Gorge, an 85 mile circuit from Christchurch, is famed for trout and salmon fishing. From the Main West Road through Darfield and Sheffield, cross the Waimakariri River to the Gorge. Try a Waimakariri or Rakaia jetboat or a raft tour for half a day, a day or two days. Rafting tours also operate on the Waiau, Hurunui and Rangitata Rivers. (North of Oxford, follow the turn-off to the Ashley River Gorge, returning to Christchurch via Rangiora and Belfast.)

Salmon fishing in the Rakaia, Rangitata and Waimakariri Rivers is from 1 October to 30 April, with the best runs in December-March, October-December are noted for sea-run trout in all local rivers, and brown trout throughout the season. Rainbow and brown trout, landlocked salmon, and brook trout are found in Lakes Taylor, Sumner, Coleridge,

Lyndon and Selfe from early November to the end of April.
Excellent sea fishing is available around river mouths. Kawhai
(Australian salmon) and cod are the main species caught. For
the best locations for river, lake and sea fishing, use the
services of one of the many excellent local fishing guides.

Mt. Hutt ski area has the longest and most reliable ski
season in New Zealand, and offers a 'snow guarantee'. Snow
conditions range from powder in early winter to corn in late
spring. 75 per cent of the skiing terrain of its huge basin is
rated 'learner-intermediate', but advanced skiing in the back
bowls is outstanding. Heliskiing is some of the best in the
world.

Methven, the winter resort serving Mt. Hutt ski area (late
May through early December), also operates as a base for
mountaineering, deer hunting and fishing. Within an hour's
drive of Methven are three major rivers and numerous lakes.
The Rakaia Gorge (a 100 mile circuit), 10 miles north of
Methven, is very picturesque. Follow Highway 72 to Darfield
via scenic Glentunnel, returning to Christchurch via the Main
West Road.

TOUR 14

CHRISTCHURCH—QUEENSTOWN

Drive from Christchurch through alpine foothills over Burke's
Pass to glacial lakes mirroring Mt. Cook National Park's
mountains. Pass through only a handful of holiday villages in
Mackenzie Valley, catering to skiers and sportsmen, then over
the winding Lindis Pass road down to magnificent vistas of
the Queenstown area.

Suggested schedule

7:00 a.m.	Breakfast and check out.
7:30 a.m.	Hire a car for the drive around South Island and depart for Mt. Cook.
12:00 noon	Lunch in Mt. Cook Village.
1:00 p.m.	Walk from the village, scenic drive and walk to Blue Lakes (or) flightseeing to Tasman Glacier.
2:30 p.m.	Leave for Lake Ohau.
4:00 p.m.	Refreshments at the Ohau Lodge.
4:30 p.m.	Leave for Lindis Pass and Queenstown.
7:30 p.m.	Arrive in Queenstown and check in.
8:30 p.m.	Dinner. Stroll around the Queenstown Mall and lakefront.

Christchurch to Mt. Cook

The South Canterbury and North Otago provinces are
separated by the Waitaki River, parallelled by Highway 83
and, from Kurow, Highway 82 linking Lake Benmore, New
Zealand's largest man-made lake, to Oamaru and the east
coast. Both provinces in this region look much alike:
prosperous farming lands, vivid green in spring and brown at
the end of summer.

Driving south across sheep-covered plains from
Christchurch to Timaru is a monotonous 2½-hour trip,
usually best seen from the air as a pattern of pastures,
farmland, rivers and streams ascending foothills to the Alps.
The same is true of the 1½-hour trip from Timaru south to
Oamaru. Instead, leave Highway 1 at Geraldine for Highway
79, through Fairlie, Burke's Pass and the beautiful Lake
Pukaki, a deep milky blue from glacial minerals. Then turn
north along Highway 80, parallelling Lake Pukaki to Mt.
Cook. From there it's a four-hour drive to Queenstown on

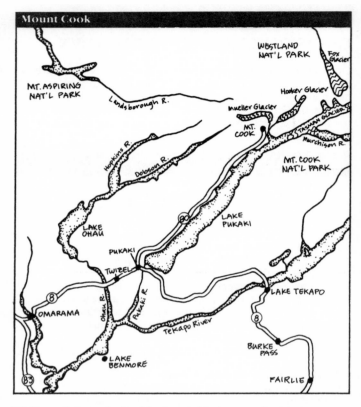

Highway 8 through the Mackenzie Basin over the bleak
tussock-covered hills of Lindis Pass.

Sightseeing highlights
●●●**Mt. Cook** is the highest mountain in New Zealand
(12,349 feet), surrounded by 140 peaks over 7,000 feet.
Between the mountains are glaciers, including the Tasman (18
miles long and two miles wide), the largest outside the
Himalayas and Antarctica. In winter, Mt. Cook offers
excellent skiing: glacier, heliskiing, alpine, nordic and ski
mountaineering. Walkers and climbers will find the Mt.
Cook National Park to be a feast of scenery and native
plants, including beautiful wild flowers from October to
January. Stop at the Mt. Cook National Park Headquarters
(tel. 818) in Mt. Cook Village for Park information.

Even a ten- to 30-minute walk from the village will reveal the park's great natural beauty. For a combination of a scenic drive and a short walk, take Highway 80 to Ball Hut Road, the Tasman Valley Road, a gravel road that follows the Tasman River and glacier to the car-park at Husky Flats. Follow the sign to Blue Lakes and in 15 minutes you have a grand view of the lakes. A few more minutes up the Clacker View Track for tremendous views of Tasman Glacier, Mt. Tasman and Mt. Cook.

For hikers there are several excellent 2- to 2½-hour walks: Kea Point, Sealy Tarns and Red Tarns. The Hooker Valley Trail leads over Copeland Pass to Fox Glacier (only for hikers with alpine experience in ice and snow, the right equipment and a guide). From Mt. Cook, light planes fly over the divide to Fox and Franz Josef Glaciers. The Helicopter Line offers a 20-minute flight around Mt. Cook for NZ$50 (£20) and 45 minutes with a snow landing for NZ$125 (£50) per person (tel. Mt. Cook 855). A 30-minute Mt. Cook Line flight landing on snow is NZ$100 (£40) (tel. Mt. Cook 849).

The Hermitage Hotel's travel desk (tel. 809) can book any activities in the area. Mt. Cook Line buses connect with Christchurch (NZ$34 (£13.50)) and Queenstown (NZ$34 (£13.50)). Mt. Cook Airlines fly in two or three times a day from Christchurch (NZ$125.40 (£50)) depending on the season. Newmans Airlines flies into Glentanner Airport (on the shores of Lake Pukaki, about 20 miles south of the Village) from Christchurch, Wanaka and Queenstown (tel. 855 in Mt. Cook for latest schedules and fares).

A sumptuous smorgasbord lunch in the Alpine Room of the world famous THC Hermitage (tel. 809), or a snack in the Coffee Bar, is something special to look forward to after the drive from Christchurch. Stay at the THC-owned Mt. Cook Chalets (tel. 809), NZ$60 (£24) single or double, or the new YHA Hostel (tel. 820) at NZ$12 (£4.80), if you find it too hard to leave the Mt. Cook area after just half a day.

●**The Mackenzie Basin**'s vast tussock-covered expanses can seem barren and monotonous in winter, but the spectacular backdrop of the Southern Alps adds dramatic beauty to the trip.

●●**Lakes Tekapo and Pukaki** acquire blue-green and turquoise colours from fine dust created by glacial grinding that feeds into their waters. In summer Lake Tekapo's shores are covered with bluish purple, pink and yellow lupins. In winter (July to late October) Lake Tekapo has a large beginners' ski area and a ski school catering to novices. Nordic skiing on the Hooker and Tasman Riverflats or on the

glaciers and heliskiing flights to the six- to eight-mile-long
runs of the Tasman Glacier are available from the local
airfield. Contact Alpine Guides in Mt. Cook (tel. 834) or
Alpine Recreation Canterbury in Lake Tekapo (tel. 736) for
latest information, costs and bookings.

●●**Lake Ohau** west on Highway 8 between Twizel and
Omarama, 1½ hours from Mt. Cook, is a beautiful place for
fishing, boating, hiking and skiing. Nearby Mt. Sutton has
superb heliski runs. Below the mountain, Lake Ohau Lodge
provides luxury accommodation at only NZ$60 (£24) double.

Where to stay: Queenstown

The **YHA Hostel**, 80 Esplanade, tel. 352, is worth booking
well in advance to ensure one of the best low-budget (NZ$8
(£3.20)) lakeside lodgings in the world, assuming that you
don't mind the curfew. The next best choices for budgeteers
are: cabins, NZ$18 (£7) depending on facilities, or campsites
in the **Queenstown Holiday Park**, tel. 29-306, at Arthur's
Point; tourist flats (NZ$38–$50 (£15–£20) two people) or
campsites in the **Queenstown Motor Park**, tel. 27-254, and
the **Mountain View Lodge Holiday Park**, Frankton Road,
tel. 28-246, primarily a motel but with upper and lower
tent-sites, NZ$36 (£14.50) for two people; and in Frankton,
cabins, NZ$20–$30 (£8–£12) for two people, tent or caravan
sites at the **Frankton Motor Camp**, tel. 27-247, and
Kawarau Falls Holiday Camp, tel. 27-323.

The **Aroha Flats**, 20 Hay Street, tel. 27-777, three
minutes' walk from the mall, with very spacious rooms and
picture-postcard views of town and the lake, charging only
NZ$39 (£15.50) for two people is about the best value in
Queenstown. If you have a car, the **Lake Hayes Motel**,
Lakes Hayes Road, tel. AW705, literally on the shores of the
beautiful Lake Hayes, is a wonderful respite at NZ$47 (£19)
for two people.

A notch up in budget, B&B at NZ$48 (£19.50) for two
people, the **Wakatipu Lodge**, in Frankton at 25 Stewart
Street, tel. 23-037, has free shuttle service to Queenstown.
For accommodation not too far from the centre of town, with
views and full facilities, the **Goldfields Guesthouse B&B**,
41 Frankton Road, tel. 27-211, is a bargain at NZ$49–$54
(£20–£21.50) for two people. If these rooms are booked, ask
about their B&B motel flats at NZ$58 (£23) for two people.

The **Mountain View Lodge**, tel. 28-246, in Frankton
Road competes with these prices, NZ$58 (£23) for two
people. Many other good motels are in the same price range,
including the **Alpine Village Motor Inn**, Frankton Road,

tel. 27-795, with great lakeside views, heated pools and a
shuttle service; the **Four Seasons Motel**, 12 Standley Street,
tel. 28-953; the **Holloways Motel**, Lake Esplanade, tel.
28-002, which matches views with the best; the very pretty
A-1 Queenstown Motel, 13 Frankton Road, tel. 27-289 with
a private spa pool; and **Amber Motor Lodge**, Shotover
Street, tel. 28-480.

In the luxury category, the **Travelodge**, Beach Street, tel.
27-800, may have captured the best location in town, but for
better value for the money, NZ$145–$165 (£58–£66), **The
Lofts**, tel. 27-391, on nearby Shotover Street, offers class,
comfort and intimacy.

Itinerary options: Dunedin—Otago Peninsula—Stewart Island

Dunedin and the Otago Peninsula is an itinerary option
requiring at least three days of driving and touring time
between Christchurch and Queenstown. There is no direct
way to drive from Dunedin to Queenstown, only
Dunedin-Ranfurly-Alexandra-Cromwell-Queenstown or
Dunedin-Milton-Raes Junction-Alexandra-Cromwell-
Queenstown. Either route requires a six-hour drive.

Dunedin: Fuelled by Central Otago's gold rush in the
1860s, Dunedin became Victorian New Zealand's wealthiest
town. 'The Edinburgh of the South' envisaged by its Scottish
founders flourished as a planned city with more interesting,
diverse architecture than any other in the country. Dunedin is
framed by a green belt on the hills facing the harbour set
between the rugged Otago Peninsula and the coast.

North of the city, Signal Hill and Mount Cargill offer
sweeping panoramas of the harbour, or follow the four-mile
Queens Drive through the Town Belt. Other viewpoints
include Unity Park, Bracken's Lookout, Southern Cemetery
and Prospect Park.

The 35-room Jacobean-style Olveston Mansion, Dunedin's
primary attraction, is a showcase of European antiques only
matched by the Lanarch Castle on Otago Peninsula.

The Otago Peninsula: This is the third of New Zealand's
extraordinary peninsulas, the others being Coromandel and
Banks. The Otago Peninsula, north-east of Dunedin, offers
high-contrast scenery between the Otago Harbour and Pacific
Ocean sides: serene and dotted with settlements on the
harbour side, wild and rugged on the ocean side.

Larnarch Castle (1871), a 43-room neo-gothic 'monument'
set in 35 acres of gardens, contains a 3,000 sq. ft. ballroom
crafted and furnished in grand style. Richly carved ceilings

and Venetian glass, created by imported European craftsmen, decorate the rooms. The Tower, over 1,000 feet above sea level, provides superb views of the peninsula and harbour.

The Royal Albatross Colony is the closest nesting place to a developed area for these huge birds. The breeding grounds can be visited by prior arrangement, from November to September, with December to May the best viewing months. Chicks hatch in January.

Yellow-eyed penguins come ashore to nest in Penguin Bay and seals bask on a rocky islet (Seal Island) only 10 yards from shore.

Stewart Island: You need a good reason for driving the 3½ hours from Dunedin to Invercargill (plus at least three more hours if you follow the south-eastern coastal route). For nature lovers, the very good reason is Stewart Island.

From Bluff on the ferry *MV Wairua*, Stewart Island is two hours across the Foveaux Strait (or 20 minutes by air). With its brilliant dawns and sunsets, the Maoris call it Rakiura— 'Island of the Glowing Sky'. Most of the 500 people on this unspoiled 40-mile by 25-mile (425,000 acre) island, descendants of European whalers, live in Halfmoon Bay (Oban) and fish the often stormy Pacific and Antarctic waters. Visit the Rakiura Museum for Stewart Island's history.

With only 12½ miles of road on the northern coast, this is an island for walkers, birdwatchers, and deer hunters. Bring waterproof clothing and boots. In particular, this island is an ornithologist's paradise: tui and bellbirds in spring, tomtit and rare wekas in summer, fantails in winter, and parakeets, kakas, fernbirds, dotterels, brown creepers, moreporks, and perhaps even kiwis all year round.

Launch cruise charters and self-charters visit Ulva Island's sandy beaches and wooded walking trails, Paterson Inlet, Ocean Beach, Port Adventure and Port William. Enjoy short walks to Horseshoe Bay, Garden Mound, Ringoringa Beach and Lee Bay. The northern part of the island offers weeks of hiking, but obtain local information and maps first, and avoid wandering off the beaten track.

The **South Sea Hotel** (tel. 6), a B&B for NZ$35 (£14), **Rakiura Motel** (tel. 275) at NZ$45 (£18) for two people, **Horseshoe Haven**'s (tel. 56K) A-frame units at NZ$31 (£12.50) for two and a lodge at NZ$11 (£4.40) per person, and **Ferndale Caravan Park** (tel. 52M) at NZ$35 (£14) for two people are all the accommodation you'll find on the island except for forestry huts, a few campsites, and private homes that make rooms available to holiday-makers.

TOUR 15

QUEENSTOWN

Board the *S.S. Earnslaw* for a mid-morning cruise on Lake
Wakatipu to a lakeside working sheep station. After returning
to Queenstown, visit Arrowtown for lunch as a leisurely start
to a memorably exciting afternoon of jetboating on the
Shotover River and four-wheel driving, or possibly
pony-trekking, to catch the sunset.

Suggested schedule

8:00 a.m.	Lakeside snack breakfast. Sightseeing and shopping in the Queenstown Mall.
10:00 a.m.	*S.S. Earnslaw* cruise (with more breakfast) to Mt. Nicholas Sheep Station.
12:00 noon	Drive or bus to Arrowtown for sightseeing and lunch, with a side trip up Coronet Peak for the view.
3:00 p.m.	Shotover jetboat trip.
8:00 p.m.	Dinner and relaxation on Bob's Peak. Spend the night in Queenstown or Frankton.

Orientation

Queenstown is the South Island's, New Zealand's and one of
the world's most outstanding recreational resorts. The variety
of spectacular year-round lake, mountain and river
recreational attractions in the region, including Queenstown,
Te Anau, Fiordland National Park, Wanaka and Mt. Aspiring
National Park, is unsurpassed anywhere. Nestled at the head
of a small bay on Lake Wakatipu (52 miles long), surrounded
by rugged mountains rising steeply from the shoreline,
Queenstown is a compact town easily toured on foot. Using
Queenstown as a base, after arriving you can book a seemingly
unlimited variety of excursions: white-water rafting, jetboats,
cruise trips, hydrofoil rides, four-wheel drive and horseback
trips, climbing, hiking, camping, skiing (mostly downhill and
heliskiing), fishing, and combinations thereof, with guides and
helicopter transport options, from a half-day to a week or
more.

   The more popular excursions fill rapidly, especially during
peak tourist months, so be prepared to make booking

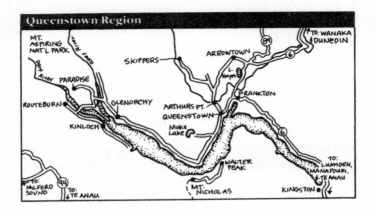

decisions as soon as you arrive in town. The NZTP Travel
Office (tel. 143) in Shotover Street can fill all your
information and booking requirements for lake and river trips,
horseback trips, flightseeing excursions to Milford Sound, and
accommodation from Te Anau to Wanaka.

Sightseeing highlights

●●●**Lake Wakatipu** deserves a leisurely cruise or launch
trip for one to three hours. The *S.S. Earnslaw*, a completely
renovated coal-burning steamship that made her debut on the
lake in 1912, sails several times a day (NZ$19 (£7.60) adult,
NZ$9.50 (£3.80) child) to the Mt. Nicholas Sheep Station for
a sheep-shearing demonstration. Cross the lake by launch
(NZ$17 (£6.80) adult, NZ$8.50 (£3.40) child) to the Cecil
Peak Sheep and Cattle Station (soon to have a major resort
development). The hydrofoil *Meteor III* takes passengers on a
25-mile cruise to the upper reaches of the lake (NZ$22
(£8.80) adult, NZ$11 (£4.40) child) and offers a 20-minute
mini-cruise (NZ$10 (£4) adult, NZ$7.50 (£3) child).
●●●**The Shotover and Kawarau Rivers** offer the
ultimate in white-water rafting and jetboating. Jetboat from
Queenstown down the lake to the Kawarau River and then
downriver. Shoot incredible white-water rapids through the
narrow canyon of the Shotover River and then raft through
the Upper Kawarau. Rafting trips range from NZ$40 (£16) to
NZ$90 (£36) per person, jetboat trips NZ$30 (£12) adult,
NZ$15 (£6) child. Helicopter flights will take you to and from
the rivers on flightseeing trips and even drop you off at the
top of Bob's Peak (NZ$85 (£34) per person). White-water

hovercraft trips are available for those who would rather whisk through the foaming rapids on a cushion of air in an enclosed cabin (NZ$50 (£20) per person).

● ●**Arrowtown** is a pretty village of old wood and stone cottages nestling beneath sycamore trees, the relic of a gold mining boom that brought thousands of miners to the Arrow and Shotover Rivers. The Lake District Centennial Museum in Arrowtown contains one of the country's best gold-mining sections.

● ●**Coronet Peak**, 12 miles north of Queenstown on the way to Arrowtown, has a chair-lift to the summit station for a magnificent panoramic view of Lake Wakatipu and the Southern Alps. In winter, from mid-June to October, Coronet Peak and the Remarkables give Queenstown two of the most challenging skiing terrains in the Southern Hemisphere. Even if you don't ski, the views of surrounding mountains and lakes from the Remarkables' access road is worth the trip (put on chains in the winter).

● ●**Bob's Peak** and its Skyline Restaurant, reached by a four-minute (1,530-foot) gondola ride (NZ$5.50 (£2.20) adult, NZ$1.50 (£0.60) child) starting near the town centre is the best and easiest way to see the town and its surroundings on a clear day or night.

Where to eat

After a day of jetboating, white-water rafting or other adventurous and vigorous activity, any food will look and smell great. Add a touch of ambience, charm or a roaring fireplace on a cool night and it can seem brilliant. Restaurants in Queenstown that qualify for this description are: pizzas and spaghetti dishes at the cosy **Cow Restaurant**, tel. 567, in Cow Lane; **Sablis**, Arcade in Beach Street, tel. 145, for a wide variety of meat and poultry dishes; **Upstairs Downstairs**, 66 Shotover Street, tel. 203; and next door, New Zealand's traditional meat and poultry cuisine at **Roaring Megs**, 57 Shotover Street, tel. 968, with candlelight (you will need to dress up). You shouldn't miss eating, drinking or both at the **Skyline**, tel. 123, on Bob's Peak in Queenstown, reached by cable car. The food may not be remarkable, but the view is.

By and large, stick to tasty budget meals in Queenstown, such as **Twenty Minutes** in the mall, the **Gourmet Express Restaurant and Coffee Shop** in the Bay Centre in Shotover Street, the **Rees Cafe** in Rees Place Arcade, the **Remarkable Food Establishment** in Rees Street, and **Cobb & Co.**, corner of Rees and Beach Streets.

Westy's on the Mall, tel. 609, serves excellent food at inflated prices. **Packer's Arms**, tel. 929, is a very expensive dining 'experience' in an historic building on Arthur's Point. If you get cold feet, try **Arthur's Point Pub and Restaurant** for seafood or steaks and nightly specials.

The Flash in the Pan, The Mall, Buckingham Street, tel. 828, in Arrowtown serves a decent lunch.

Itinerary options

Skippers Canyon is about four hours return by mini-coach or four-wheel-drive vehicle from Queenstown (NZ$26.50 (£10.50) adult, NZ$13 (£5.20) child). The narrow, single-lane road that snakes high above the Shotover River is unforgettable, especially on a winter trip! A three-hour horseback ride up the Shotover and Moonlight Valleys leaves at 9:30 a.m. and 2:00 p.m. from **Moonlight Stables**, NZ$28.50 (£11.50). A three-hour ride through Arrow River Gorge from **Hunters Horse Trekking** leaves at the same times and costs the same.

TOUR 16

QUEENSTOWN—TE ANAU

Te Anau, near the southern end of the largest of the region's
lakes, is the gateway and touring base for excursions to
Milford and Doubtful Sounds and Lake Manapouri. The
120-mile trip from Queenstown on Highways 6 and 94
through Lumsden and sheep and cattle country should take
no more than three hours.

Suggested schedule

7:00 a.m.	Early breakfast in Queenstown.
8:00 a.m.	Check out and leave for Te Anau.
11:00 a.m.	Check in at Te Anau. Confirm Milford and other bookings.
12:00 noon	Picnic lunch at Lake Te Anau.
1:00 p.m.	Half-day launch trip to West Arm.
6:30 p.m.	Leisurely dinner and early to bed.

Sightseeing highlights

●●●**Fiordland National Park**, New Zealand's largest and
most remote park, covers over three million acres of the
south-western South Island. Take the main road out of
Queenstown to Frankton, then go south on Highway 6 along
the Remarkables through Kingston to just before Lumsden,
where Highway 94 branches west to the towns of Te Anau
and Manapouri, just outside the park's boundary, and
Fiordland National Park. Gaze in wonderment at the still
waters of deep glacier-formed fiords broken only by seals,
dolphins and penguins. Towering waterfalls tumble from
sheer 4,500-foot walls. Mountain peaks are reflected in deep
blue lakes dotted with forest-covered islands. Crystal clear
rivers, powered by seemingly endless days of rain or drizzle,
flow from rugged, snow-capped and often mist-shrouded
mountains covered with dense green beech forests that shelter
the blue and iridescent green takahe and the nocturnal,
flightless kiwi, weka and kakapo, some of the world's rarest
birds. These unique sightseeing experiences are unsurpassed
anywhere on earth, even on gloomy, overcast Fiordland days.
Winter—June to August—is the best time for clear views and
relatively little rain. The road to Milford is open in winter,
but the higher areas are subject to heavy snowfalls. In

summer, prepare (with your favourite insect repellant) for the
fly in the Fiordland's ointment: tiny ferocious black sandflies
that inflict painful, itchy bites, especially around dusk.

● ●**Lake Manapouri**, which tends to be overlooked in
relation to Lake Wakatipu and Te Anau, may be New
Zealand's most beautiful lake, as well as the deepest (1,500
feet). The lake contains 30 picturesque islets. Stockyard Cove
is a lovely spot for picnics. Take a launch tour to the West
Arm to visit the hydro-electric powerhouse 700 feet under a
mountain. Water from the lake plunges through turbines and
then along a six-mile tunnel into Doubtful Sound. From the
tunnel a bus travels over the 2,200 foot Wilmot Pass to Deep
Cove. Then board a two-hour launch cruise on Doubtful
Sound, ten times larger than Milford Sound, with waterfalls
cascading hundreds of feet. A full-day's coach trip, including
the cruise, costs NZ$55 (£22).

Where to stay

Budget travellers will appreciate Te Anau's **YHA Hostel**,
Milford Road, tel. 7847, one of the most attractive in New
Zealand, about a mile from town (NZ$8 (£3.20)).

Inexpensive camping sites and cabins are available at
various distances from Te Anau. The **Mountain View
Cabin and Caravan Park** has cabins for NZ$18 (£7) for
two people. **Te Anau Motor Park**, Manapouri Highway, tel.
7457, about half a mile from town, costs NZ$5 (£2) per
person and also has cabins and chalets, NZ$17–$48 (£7–£19)
for two people, and caravan sites. Outside Manapouri, 12
miles south of Te Anau, the **Lakeview Motor Park**, Te
Anau Road, tel. 624, has cabins at NZ$18 (£7) for two
people; and, on a beautiful lakeside site, the **Manapouri
Glade Caravan Park**'s cabins charge NZ$15 (£6) for two
people, tel. 623.

Among B&Bs, the **Matai Lodge**, Matai Street, tel. 7360, is
one of the few with doubles under NZ$50 (£20). Among
motels, only the **XL Motel**, Te Anau Terrace, tel. 7258, has
rates under NZ$50 (£20) for doubles. There are numerous
motels in the NZ$50–$60 (£20–£24) range.

Where to eat

Considering the number of tourists heading for Milford
Sound, Te Anau could do with more eating places in the
budget- and medium-price categories. Except for those that
may be opening as I'm writing, the choices for decent,
nothing-fancy fare include: the **Coffee Shop** in Main Street;
Vacation Inn, The Gallery; the **Luxmore Motor Lodge** in

Milford Road, and **Bailey's** next door; **Light Bight** on the
lakefront; and **Pop-in Catering** in Te Anau Terrace for
breakfasts and hot meals. The only somewhat fancier and
higher-priced eating place is the **Grubsteak Restaurant** at
the THC Te Anau Hotel in Te Anau Terrace.

Itinerary options
Take a ten-minute helicopter flight to Mt. Luxmore and over
Lake Manapouri for NZ$35 (£14) or one of a dozen other
chopper and floatplane trips over the region at prices that
start at NZ$25 (£10) per person up to NZ$200 (£80). **Air
Fiordland** (tel. 7505), **Waterwings Airways** (tel. 7405) or
Fiordland Flights (tel. 7799) will arrange these flights and
pick you up in Te Anau, or you can drive out to the Te Anau
Airfield south of town.

Hiking and skiing in the Southern Alps
Fiordland National Park and Mt. Aspiring National Park
contain incredibly beautiful terrain, both tame and wild. The
rugged, snow-capped mountain ranges, dense rain forests,
alpine lakes and rivers, waterfalls and majestic fiords, offer a
marvellous variety of rambling and hiking of varying
difficulty. Reached from Te Anau and Queenstown, the
Milford Track, Routeburn Walk, Hollyford Valley Walk and
Greenstone Valley Walk range from difficult to easy and none
requires more than good physical fitness, comfortable and
waterproof gear, and adequate time.

The Milford Track, a 35-mile trail, is New Zealand's
best-known walk. Highlights of the track are views from
MacKinnon Pass, the 1,800-foot Sutherland Falls, the
incredible variety of rain forest, and the torrents of water
cascading everywhere after rain.

With an early morning departure to Te Anau from
Queenstown, the Milford Track takes five days (including an
arrival day in Queenstown). Open from early November to
early April, a permit is necessary from the Park Headquarters
in Te Anau. For independent hikers, an NZRR bus leaves Te
Anau for the 45-minute journey to Te Anau Downs at 1:15
p.m., connecting with the boat to Glade House. Each of the
next three days of walking is divided into 10- to 13-mile
segments, followed by hot showers and meals at Pompolona
Lodge and then Quintin Hut. At the end of the trail, a boat
leaves Sandfly Point at 2:00 p.m. and 4:00 p.m. for Milford.
If you do not plan to catch the 3:00 p.m. bus to Te Anau, you
should know that the next bus leaves at 7:45 a.m.

The Hollyford Valley Walk is a way to combine walking,

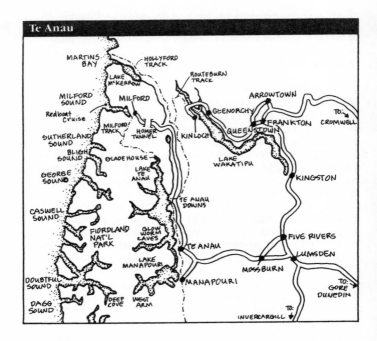

river jetboating and flightseeing to Milford Sound, the scenic
drive from Milford to Te Anau, and fishing for trout and
kahawai. From late October to mid-April, walk along the
broad Hollyford Valley to the Tasman Sea at Martin's Bay
(four-day trip), departing on a scenic flight to Milford Sound
or flightsee over Milford and Routeburn tracks; or a five-day
trip alternative including a jetboat on Lake McKerrow.
Contact **Hollyford Tourist & Travel Ltd.**, Invercargill, tel.
44300. The walk-in/walk-out tour is 24 miles; walk-in/fly-out
is 16 miles; with optional side-trips of another 12 miles; or 55
miles of a jetboating option. For a much easier walk than
Milford or Hollyford, the 22-mile Greenstone Valley Walk
has much to offer. The trail passes the beautiful lakes
Howden and McKellar, then follows the Greenstone River to
Lake Wakatipu. Greenstone is one of the walks that can be
done all year but October to April is the best time. Much less
well known than the Milford Track, the Routeburn Walk is
nonetheless one of the best rain forest/sub alpine trails in the
world. Spanning two magnificent national parks, the 25-mile
trail starts and finishes about 1,500 feet above sea level, with a

great variety of scenery and flora. Highlights of the trip are
views from Harris Saddle (4,200 feet) and Key Summit. The
higher elevations mostly eliminate the sandfly problem that
plagues the Milford Track. The keen hiker can combine a
Hollyford and Routeburn walk. Often the Greenstone Walk is
used as the return to Queenstown from Routeburn. At Elfin
Bay you can charter a jetboat to Queenstown or walk to
Kinloch to meet the bus to Routeburn.

Routeburn Walk Ltd., Queenstown, tel. 100, offers a guided
walk, with transport from Queenstown, accommodation and
meals, for about NZ$350 (£140) per adult. An advantage of
this tour is that Routeburn Falls and Lake Mackenzie Lodges
are available exclusively for this tour.

Skiing in the Southern Alps: The scenery is stunningly
beautiful and virtually unmarked by resort or other
development. The ski lifts and slopes are comparatively
uncrowded. Waiting at lifts is uncommon. You spend most of
your time skiing, even at weekends. Lift tickets, equipment
hire, excellent ski instruction, accommodation, and après-ski
activities can cost about half as much as in Europe. Returning
from the ski mountains, if there's time you can engage in
virtually all of the other year-round activities mentioned
above. Sounds too good to be true? Except for a very rare lack
of snow, in the Queenstown-Wanaka region it's all true.

Close to Queenstown, Coronet Peak has excellent skiing at
all levels, especially advanced and intermediate, with one of
the best ski schools in New Zealand. Lift tickets are
interchangeable with the Remarkables. The Remarkables have
more excellent beginner and intermediate trails than Coronet.
There are cross-country ski trails above the lifts and telemark
instruction is available.

The Harris Mountains are New Zealand's leading heliskiing
area with over 140 runs from 40 different peaks in three
mountain ranges. Experienced and advanced skiers can have
12,000 feet of awe-inspiring runs in the Tyndall Glaciers and
Buchanan Range. The cost is about NZ$350 (£140) per day
or about NZ$16 (£6.50) per 1,000 vertical feet.

Treble Cone, 18 miles from Wanaka, deserves to be much
better known for its skiing and scenery. A skier chalet at the
top of the double chairlift offers spectacular views of
surrounding mountains. Many of the Harris Mountain
heliskiing trips begin from Treble Cone. Cardrona is the
South Island's most promising new ski area. A high base
elevation (4,500 feet) and southerly exposure provide ample
snow coverage in the June-November season.

TOUR 17

TE ANAU—MILFORD SOUND

Start very early on a full-day trip from Te Anau to the fabulous Milford Sound, including a three-hour drive over The Divide and through Homer Tunnel to the end of the road at THC Milford Resort Hotel, then a cruise through Milford Sound to see pyramid-shaped Mitre Peak, Stirling Falls and several other magnificent waterfalls arching into the Sound from high sheer walls and hanging valleys.

Suggested schedule

7:00 a.m.	Breakfast in Te Anau.
8.30 a.m.	Drive to Milford Sound with sightseeing stops at lakes along the way.
12:00 noon	Launch cruise on Milford Sound.
2:30 p.m.	Return to Te Anau.
3:00 p.m.	Te Ana-au Caves Tour.
5:00 p.m.	Return to Te Anau for an early dinner.

Transport

Te Anau to Milford Sound is a three-hour drive by way of Eglinton and Hollyford Valleys and Homer Tunnel. It's 60 miles through beech forests surrounded by high rugged peaks. The high rainfall creates dark green beech forests covering thick fern, shrub, rich carpets of spongy moss and peat, and other plant growth, even on steep rock faces. Start driving early to Milford on Highway 94 (Milford Road) to avoid the mountains clouding up or bad weather. A call to Park Headquarters (tel. 7521) at 8:00 a.m. for the weather report would be sensible. Be sure to wear or bring waterproof and warm gear. The first 18 miles of the road skirts the shores of Lake Te Anau, then follows the Eglinton River flanked by beech forests. On the way through Eglinton Valley to The Divide, the 1,500-foot pass over the Southern Alps, Mirror Lakes (about 25 miles) and the beautiful Lake Gunn (about 50 miles) are worthwhile stopping places. Although little more than ponds, Mirror Lakes yield perfect reflections of surrounding peaks. Climb the forested ridge to Cascade Creek which, in addition to accommodation and refreshments, has views of many waterfalls cascading from bush-covered valley

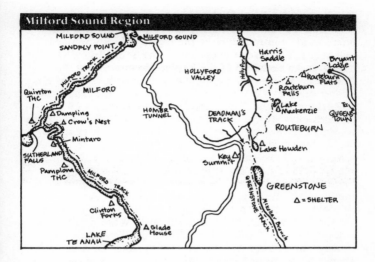

Milford Sound Region

walls. Then drive over The Divide, eight miles before Homer
Tunnel, the starting point of the Routeburn and Greenstone
tracks to Lake Wakatipu. From Hollyford Road to Homer
Tunnel, pass through the beech forest and tussock river flats
of Hollyford Valley, some of the best scenery on the trip.
Named after Harry Homer, who discovered the Homer
Saddle in 1889, the 3,600-foot-long Homer Tunnel, begun in
1935, wasn't completed until 1953. The eastern entrance to
Homer Tunnel is 8,100 feet in elevation, descending through
the tunnel to 2,700 feet. The Cleddau Valley at the far end of
the tunnel was carved through rock by the raging waters of
the Cleddau River. At the end of the Milford trip, through
the Cleddau Valley, is a one-to-two hour Milford Sound
launch cruise with fabulous views of Mitre Peak and Stirling
Falls.

NZRRS and Fiordland Travel run regular bus services
from Te Anau for NZ13 (£5.20) single or NZ$20 (£8) return.
The coach excursion leaves at 8:15 a.m. and returns at 5:45
p.m. Both the THC and Fiordland Travel operate launch
trips on Milford Sound. With a lunch on board, the longer
cruise costs NZ$20 (£8).

One option to consider is Te Anau-Milford by bus and
return by air to either Te Anau or Queenstown. Fly with Mt.
Cook Airlines (NZ$80 (£32) per adult) or take a short flight
to the mouth of the Sound for NZ$30 (£12).

Sightseeing highlights

● ●**Lake Te Anau**, branching into three landlocked fiords, offers an ideal introduction to the region's thickly wooded mountains. The glacier-gouged lake, the South Island's largest, has a backdrop of the Kepler Mountains and the Murchison Range running parallel to the north. 'Te Anau' is a short version of a Maori word, *Te Ana-Au*, meaning 'Caves of Rushing Waters'. The myriad mysterious shapes of greenish glow-worms gleaming from 15,000 years of limestone accretions have made these recently discovered caves across the lake one of the most popular local attractions. Te Ana-Au Caves can only be reached by boat, costing NZ$21 (£8.50) adult, NZ$8 (£3.20) child. Book this 2½-hour trip at the Fiordland Travel Centre (at the intersection of Milford Road and Te Anau Terrace, tel. 7416) which, besides Park Headquarters, is the main source of travel information for the Te Anau-Manapouri-Milford Sound area. While you're there, pick up NZ$.50 (£0.20) tokens to visit the Te Anau Underground Trout Observatory, south along Te Anau Terrace across from Park Headquarters, where you can watch, feed and photograph brown, rainbow and native trout daily from 6:00 a.m. to 9:45 p.m. To find some easy walks along the lake, from the observatory continue south along Te Anau Terrace and turn right on the road along the lake toward Manapouri. Starting at the control gates, Riverside Walk and several extensions offer one- to five-hour one-way walks of varying difficulty around the lake, up Mt. Luxmore and to Lake Manapouri.

● ● ●**Milford Sound**—Cruise down the ten-mile-long, deeply furrowed glacial trough hemmed in by rock walls reaching from 900 feet underwater to almost a mile high. This fiord to the Tasman Sea passes Mitre Peak, from its reflection in the dark waters soaring over 5,000 feet straight out of the Sound; passes close enough to 450-foot Stirling Falls to feel the spray, and also Bowen Falls cascading about 500 feet from a hanging valley over two or three tiers.

Accommodation

Book well ahead at the **THC Milford Hostel** if you plan to stay overnight at Milford Sound (NZ$14 (£5.60)). The only other choice, at the head of the Fiord, is the luxurious **THC Milford Resort Hotel**, which owns the territory and charges NZ$125–$150 (£50–£60) double for the privilege of enjoying the utterly unique environment in a first-rate hotel; worth it if your budget allows.

TOUR 18

TE ANAU—QUEENSTOWN—WANAKA

Leave Te Anau early in order to take Highway 89 from
Queenstown to Wanaka and still have an active day of hiking,
boating and fishing in the Lake Wanaka area.

Suggested schedule

7:00 a.m.	Breakfast and check out.
10:30 a.m.	Highway 89 to Wanaka.
12:30 p.m.	Lunch in Wanaka.
1:30 p.m.	Walk up Mt. Iron.
2:30 p.m.	Glendhu Bay and boat trip on Lake Wanaka, or Lake Hawea for trout fishing.
7:30 p.m.	Dinner at Ripples Restaurant.

Driving from Te Anau to Westland

Retrace your driving route on Highway 94 east to Lumsden,
then north on Highway 6 to Queenstown. Lake Wanaka is
two hours from Queenstown. From Queenstown to Haast on
the west coast through Wanaka is a six-hour drive.

In good weather only (not in mid-winter!), take Highway 89
up the very steep unsurfaced road from Arrowtown to the top
of the Crown Ridge for magnificent views overlooking
Wakatipu Lake, the Kawarau River, Queenstown and the
Remarkables. This road passes through Cardrona Valley from
Wanaka to Queenstown, 44 miles of slow-going, bumpy
unsurfaced road (versus 57 miles following Highway 6 around
the Pisa Range).

Sightseeing highlights

●●● **Wanaka** is one of New Zealand's (and the world's)
most underrated resorts because it is in the shadow of
Queenstown, only 60 miles away. Lakes Wanaka and Hawea
are famed for their fishing (brown and rainbow trout and
landlocked salmon). It has the best weather and most sunshine
days in the southern lakes. Many skiers from the U.S. and
Europe prefer Treble Cone to Coronet Peak (Queenstown is
still the après-ski favourite). The Wanaka region has most of
the same outdoor recreational choices as Queenstown. For
panoramic views of Lake Wanaka and Mt. Aspiring National
Park, walk up Mt. Roy (3 hours) or Mt. Iron (1 hour). From

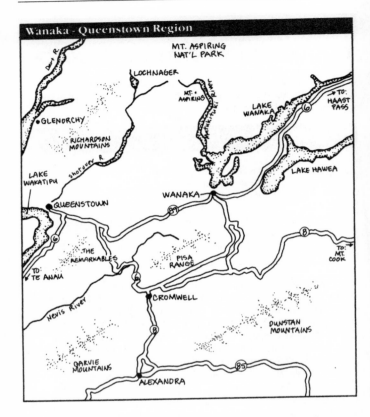

Wanaka's airfield (Mt. Aspiring Air) or from the waterfront take flightseeing excursions (NZ$20–$50 (£8–£20)) over the wilderness and lakes of Mt. Aspiring National Park, to Milford Sound (NZ$80 (£32)) and even to Mt. Cook (NZ$125 (£50)).

● ●**Glendhu Bay**, west of Wanaka and Roy's Peak on the Wanaka–Aspiring Road, especially in autumn, is renowned for its seasonal beauty and views of Mt. Aspiring National Park.

Where to stay
The **YHA Hostel**, 181 Upton Street, tel. 7405, is central, comfortable and charges NZ$10 (£4). The next cheapest accommodation, also centrally located, is at the **Wanaka Motor Camp**'s cabins, 212 Brownstone Street, tel. 7883, at NZ$30 (£12) for two people. A favourite is the **Glendhu**

Bay Camp, adjacent to Lake Wanaka, Treble Cone Road, tel. 7243, for NZ$33 (£13) for two people. Less than two miles from Wanaka, **Pleasant Lodge Caravan Park,** Mt. Aspiring Road, tel. 7360, has cabins at NZ$20 (£8) for two people, as well as caravan hire. Investigate **Penrith Park's** cabins, Beacon Point, tel. 7009, at NZ$18–$20 (£7–£8) for two people and bunkrooms in the lodge at NZ$35 (£14) for two people.

There are only a few B&Bs, with first choice the **Wanaka Lodge,** 117 Lakeside Road, tel. 7837, right on the lake with great views, for NZ$45 (£18) twin. The **Creekside Guest House,** 84 Helwick Street, tel. 7834, also costs NZ$45 (£18) double.

The half-dozen or more excellent local motels with self-contained units cost NZ$45–$60 (£18–£24) for two people. For one night, this may be the occasion when it is worth spending the extra few dollars at the **THC Wanaka,** tel. 7826, NZ$60–$90 (£24–£36), very comfortable rooms with beautiful lake and mountain views.

Where to eat
Like Te Anau, Wanaka lacks variety in budget and medium-priced restaurants. For lunch try a bistro meal at the **Storehouse Restaurant** or soup, salad and maybe pizza at **Te Kano Cafe. First Cafe** on Ardmore Street is very good but only open for dinner. The big surprise for dinner is little **Ripples Restaurant,** tel. 7413, in the Pembroke Mall, from appetizers to desserts a candidate for the prize BYO of the Southern Alps.

TOUR 19

WANAKA TO FOX AND FRANZ JOSEF GLACIERS

Leave very early once more for an eight-hour drive (including stops) from Wanaka through the Makarora Valley to Haast Pass, descending to the two great glaciers of Westland National Park, Fox and Franz Josef. Thirteen miles apart, Fox and Franz Josef Glaciers descend about six miles into rain forests 1,000 feet above sea level. The land rises to peaks over 10,000 feet high with incredible scenery. In this and the next tour, take advantage of fabulous recreational opportunities, including glacier excursions and forest walks at both glaciers.

Suggested schedule

7:00 a.m.	Breakfast and check out.
8:00 a.m.	Depart for Haast Pass.
12:00 noon	Picnic lunch near Haast Pass.
2:30 p.m.	Arrive Fox Glacier.
3:00 p.m.	Climb to Fox Chalet Lookout for sunset views.
6:30 p.m.	Depart for Franz Josef to check in, dine and relax in front of a fireplace.

Wanaka to Fox and Franz Josef Glaciers

The Haast Pass Road (Highway 6) from Wanaka to Westland National Park passes through fabulous scenery. With many one-lane bridges and gravel sections, steep slopes, blind and sharp corners, magnificent scenery and viewpoints, walking and picnicking opportunities, you can't hurry—and don't want to.

From Wanaka, continue to follow Highway 6, first along Lake Hawea and then along Lake Wanaka up the Makarora River Valley to Haast Pass. Drive through Mt. Aspiring National Park, named after the highest and most magnificent peak (over 10,000 feet), and over Haast Pass (1,700 feet). Mt. Cook is only 50 miles to the north.

Highway 6 skirts the western shore of Lake Hawea, another scenic gem known for its trout and landlocked salmon fishing, then crosses The Neck between Lakes Hawea and Wanaka, and follows Lake Wanaka to Makarora Gorge. One of the most scenic parts of the entire trip lies in Mt. Aspiring National Park, between the Gorge and Haast Pass. The mountain after which the park is named rises 10,000 feet west of Wanaka. Along Highway 6 to the 1,500-foot pass, the Makarora and other rivers flow in and out of hills and flats covered with sheep, with snow-capped peaks in the background.

From the pass, the Haast River drops through the gorge known as the Gates of Haast, where it roars through a gorge full of enormous boulders. The river is joined by the larger Landsborough in a wider valley along which you can drive down to the sea. You may want to stop in Haast, refuel and stock up on food supplies before continuing. Cross Haast Bridge and travel north 15 miles to Knights Point, a headland fringed by golden sand beaches and rocky bays, where you may see seals playing offshore just south of Lake Hoeraki, with glacial lake water and good fishing. Other good stops are two lake gems: Lake Moeraki and Lake Paringa.

Sightseeing highlights

●●●**Westland National Park**—Fox and Franz Josef Glaciers are unique in that they push steeply down into rain forest within a few miles of the sea. The park contains over 60 named glaciers and beautiful lakes. Fox and Franz Josef Glaciers can be visited easily from the Westland National Park Visitor Centres. To get to Fox Glacier from the village, backtrack south on Highway 6 a little over a mile to the Glacier Access Road. Watch for the Glacier View Road sign on the right. At the south end of the Glacier View Road starts the 40-minute Chalet Lookout Track. The Cone Rock Track branches off the Chalet Lookout Track, climbing steeply 1,000 feet above the Fox River, a strenuous hour on a steep switchback trail. The Chalet Lookout Track is much less strenuous. From Fox Glacier Hotel a walking track to the lovely Minnehaha Creek is just a 20-minute stroll through forest. Try it at night with a torch to see thousands of glow-worms dangling in the rain forest.

In Franz Josef (Tour 20), stop at the Park Centre for brochures on short walking tracks in the area and general information on hiking in the glaciers. Franz Josef Glacier is less than four miles from the Centre. Head back south along Highway 6 for a few hundred yards to the turn-off onto the Glacier Access Road. From this road through the rain-forest, many tracks branch out for 30 minutes to three or four hours of moderate to strenuous walking. The Centre's brochures provide details on all of these tracks. Don't forget to bring

rainwear and plenty of potent insect repellant in late spring
and summer months. Also plan to see at least one of the
beautiful nearby lakes—Kaniere, Mapourika, Mahinapua,
Mauapiurike, Matheson, Paring, Brunner, Ianthe or Wahapo.

Where to stay

The cost of accommodation in the Franz Josef area is lower
than in the Southern Alps, but the supply can be very short
during the summer peak season. Book ahead.

There are some excellent choices for budget watchers. The
comparatively new **Franz Josef YHA Hostel**, Cron Street,
tel. 745, costs NZ$10 (£4). The excellent **Franz Josef Motor
Camp** on the main road, tel. 766, has all facilities including a
camp shop, with cabins at NZ$15 (£6) and cottages at NZ$21
(£8.50) for two people. **Forks Motorcamp**, Okarito, tel.
Whataroa 351, 12 miles north, is in a beautiful setting, but has
only two units costing NZ$12 (£4.80) for two people.

Except for the higher-priced **THC Franz Josef**, tel. 819,
and the centrally located **Westland Motor Inn**, main road,
tel. 728, NZ$75–$95 (£30–£38) double, local motels with
lovely settings, glacier views and excellent facilities are NZ$50
(£20) and under: the **Glacier View Motel**, tel. 705,
Bushland Court Motel, Cron Street, tel. 757, and **Motel
Franz Josef**, main road, 3 miles north, tel. 742.

Where to eat

Apart from a decent sandwich at Fox Glacier's **Hobnail Cafe**
or a light meal at the **Fox Glacier Hotel**, tel. 838, either buy
and cook your own food or save your appetite and money for
Franz Josef.

In Franz Josef, the best place for grills, salads, and coffee is
D.A.'s Restaurant. Upstairs, the **Glacier Store and
Tearooms** has marvellous views of the Southern Alps. The
Westland Motor Inn, tel. 728, on the main street also has
big picture-window views of the mountains and serves
excellent light and casual meals. The **THC Franz Josef**, tel.
719, has an expensive a la carte restaurant requiring you to
dress up.

TOUR 20

FRANZ JOSEF—HOKITIKA— GREYMOUTH

Spend the morning in the Franz Josef area, then head north past scenic west coast lakes, visit a greenstone factory in Hokitika, retrace the region's gold mining era and enjoy magnificent scenery before going on to Greymouth for the night.

Suggested schedule

7:00 a.m.	Breakfast and check out.
8:00 a.m.	Franz Josef Glacier Valley Walk (or) at 9:00 a.m., the four-hour guided Franz Josef Glacier Walk (or) flightseeing trip to Tasman Glacier.
12:00 noon	Leave for a picnic lunch and lake touring *en route* to Hokitika.
2:30 p.m.	Visit Hokitika's Greenstone Factory and local sightseeing.
6:00 p.m.	Dinner in Greymouth.

Orientation

The narrow strip called Westland, never more than 30 miles wide, is yet another climatically, topographically and historically unique area of New Zealand. The last ice age, ending 14,000 years ago, covered the lowland areas that now consist of dense coniferous rain forests, alpine grasslands, shrublands, herb fields, coastal lagoons and lakes and the wide gravel beds of glacier-fed rivers. Permanent ice and snow remain above 4,500 feet, a bluish-white mass spilling slowly downward, cracking into deep ravines and crevasses under its enormous mass and the force of gravity, slowly retreating as 600 species of trees, shrubs, ferns and plants colonise the bare rocks in accordance with the altitude. The quantities of insects thriving on this kind of rain-forest and wetland environment support comparably vast numbers and varieties of birds, which you'll hear constantly chattering and singing as you walk up to the glaciers or visit some of the beautiful lakes on the 85-mile drive to Hokitika.

The weather is relatively mild, with high rainfall south of

the Westport area. Coastal growth like nikau palms and fern trees merges with coastal rain forests rising to mountain beech beneath the snow-capped peaks. The rain falls mainly at night, thereby matching Auckland for sunshine hours.

Captain Cook followed Abel Tasman on the West Coast, as he did on the North Coast of South Island. Amazingly, for 87 years after Cook's visit in 1770, the west coast wasn't approached by sea despite the hardship that Thomas Brunner and other explorers experienced on overland routes. This exploration from the Nelson area in the 1840s sought sheep and cattle country, but the discovery of gold in 1859 between Greymouth, the largest Maori settlement along the coast, and Hokitika opened a new era of settlement. Gold lured over 10,000 miners to the west coast in the next five years including an 'invasion' of Australian gold seekers. Hokitika was founded in 1864, becoming the 'Capital of the Goldfields' with a hundred hotels springing up, mostly in Revell Street. The Arthur's Pass route, discovered by Sir Arthur Dobson, was opened as a coach road in 1866, when the population of the coast surged to 50,000. Greymouth and other harbours were jammed by ships bringing new miners and supplying prospectors and storekeepers. The logging and milling of local timber and the export of bituminous coal began at the same time. Coal exports, centred around Westport to this day, expanded slowly for lack of port facilities and a railhead, and then grew rapidly after 1880 as gold mining declined in importance. The decline of gold mining left a string of deserted former boom towns – Charlestown, Barrytown, Denniston, Stockton and others. Shantytown, a historical reconstruction of a local gold settlement of the 1860s, is Greymouth's most popular attraction.

Sightseeing highlights

● ● ●**Franz Josef Glacier Valley Walk** takes you by minibus to the glacier and then on a glacier walk (2½ hours). As an alternative to the drive up the glacier there is a walking track of less than two miles on the north side of the Waiho River, going along the Callery River Gorge. At the suspension bridge where the track crosses to the Glacier Road, a second track branches off to Roberts Point above the glacier. Sentinel Rock and Peters Pool on the Glacier Road are other easily accessible vantage points, as is Canavans Knob, which begins about a mile to the south off Highway 6.

The guided **Franz Josef Glacier Walk**, offered by the THC Franz Josef Hotel, departs at 9:30 a.m. and 2:00 p.m. for a four-hour tour. Be at the hotel at 9:00 a.m. to get your

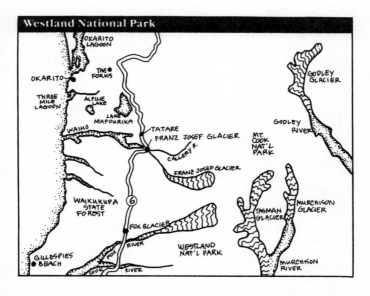

Westland National Park

special boots, socks and orientation. Experienced guides will lead you up and down icy pinnacles and over crevasses, for an unforgettable experience costing only NZ$13 (£5.20) adult, NZ$7 (£2.80) child, including all equipment. Take a snack lunch along for nourishment while on the glacier.

● ● ●**Franz Josef to Tasman Glacier flights** are offered by ski-plane or helicopter by a number of companies based in Franz Josef and Fox Glacier. The cost is NZ$40–$90 (£16–£36) per person for a 10- to 35-minute helicopter flight with Glacier Helicopters (tel. 755) or The Helicopter Line (tel. 767). For NZ$60 (£24) you can land on the snow in a 20-minute excursion with these companies or Mt. Cook Line (tel. 714).

● ●**Hokitika**'s claim to fame started with the discovery of gold in 1864. Within two years the area had 50,000 people digging for gold and more than 100 hotels. The West Coast Historical Museum in lower Tancred Street recalls the goldmining era. Today, in addition to timber milling, several factories in Hokitika cut and polish greenstone (nephrite jade) from neighbouring mountains into jewellery. Greenstone is the Maoris' sacred gemstone, for which they made perilous journeys across the Alps from the north and south. The Greenstone Factory, tel. 713, offers tours of the cutting and jewellery-making process on weekdays. Buy a souvenir rock or beautiful jewellery.

For magnificent local viewpoints, drive to the Plane Table Lookout north of Hokitika and the Sea View Lookout in a cemetery near the hospital. For a very picturesque view of the river mouth, walk down to Gibson Quay.

Take Blue Spur Road east of town to see the Vintage Farm Museum and Greenstone Factory, then visit the mine tunnels of the working Blue Spur Gold Mine. About 12 miles south of Hokitika, the Lake Kaniere Scenic Reserve offers a scenic drive and walks second to none.

Where to stay

There are plenty of reasonable accommodation choices in Greymouth. The well-equipped **Kainga-ra YHA Hostel**, Cowper Street, tel. 4951, at the south end of Greymouth has pleasant surroundings and costs the usual NZ$10 (£4).
Greymouth Seaside Motor Camp, Chesterfield Street, tel. 6618, next to the beach, can cover most of your budget needs with tent sites, caravan sites, cabins for NZ$16 (£6.40) double and flats for about NZ$30 (£12) double.

For under NZ$25 (£10) per person, stay at **Dobson Cabins** (State Highway 7 at Dobson, tel. Dobson 701) or, if you prefer a B&B, **Golden Coast Guest House**, 10 Smith Street, tel. 7839, or **West Haven Tourist Lodge**, 62 Albert Street, tel. 5605.

The **Ace Tourist Motel**, Omoto Road, tel. 6884, and the **South Beach Motel**, 318 Main South Road, tel. 26-768, are NZ$45 (£18) double. **The Kings' Motor Hotel**, 44 Mawhera Quay, tel. 5085, with a restaurant, bar and pool, is up a few notches in quality and price at NZ$60 (£24) double.

Where to eat

The best choices for light, tasty and inexpensive meals in Greymouth are **Raceway Carvery**, Union Hotel in Herbert Street, tel. 4013; the cosy **Albino Bistro** in the Kings' Motor Hotel; and the **J.B. Restaurant** in the DG Greymouth Hotel, 68 High Street, tel. 4316. For big appetites, the international menu and portions at the **West Inn**, Paroa, tel. 732, should remedy the problem.

TOUR 21

GREYMOUTH—ARTHUR'S PASS NATIONAL PARK—CHRISTCHURCH

Begin the day by visiting Shantytown, an excellent reconstruction of a gold-mining town. Then start the spectacular 100-mile trip on Arthur's Pass Road (Highway 73). Crossing The Divide affords magnificent views and opportunities to explore Arthur's Pass National Park on the way back to Christchurch. Make steep ascents and descents along the twisting pathways of four glacier-fed rivers—the Taramakau, Otira, Bealey and Waimakariri—rushing through totally contrasting landscapes of mountains and foothills on the wet western and dry eastern sides of the highest road across the Southern Alps. Scenic views and both short and longer walking or hiking trails are easily accessible from the highway.

Suggested schedule

7:00 a.m.	Breakfast and check out.
8:30 a.m.	Visit Shantytown.
9:30 a.m.	Arthur's Pass Road up to the Pass.
12:00 noon	Picnic or other lunch near Arthur's Pass Village.
1:00 p.m.	Scenic walks in the vicinity of the village.
4:00 p.m.	Descend to Christchurch.
7:00 p.m.	Dinner in Christchurch.

Sightseeing highlights
●●**Shantytown** is a faithful reconstruction of the old west coast gold mining town, complete with hotel, church, shops, jail and gallows, livery stables, steam engine, gem and mineral hall and working gold claim where visitors can pan. Open 8:30 a.m. to 5:00 p.m.

●●●**Arthur's Pass National Park** is reached from the old gold mining town of Kumaru in Westland, at the junction of Highways 6 and 73. Highway 73 traverses the Main Divide to Springfield on the western outskirts of Christchurch. As you drive along this surfaced and well-maintained road, try to imagine a thousand workers with picks and shovels building first the road and then the railway over Arthur's Pass in the

middle of winter; Cobb & Co. stage coaches madly racing for
36 hours to reach visions of fortunes to be made in Westland's
newly discovered gold fields; and Maoris using this route,
without a road, to obtain precious greenstone in the river beds
of the western mountains. Ascend steeply through lush
grassland in the Taramakau River Valley, past the old railway
town of Otira, and then cross the Otira River to Arthur's
Pass. (Between Otira and Arthur's Pass caravans and trailers
are banned. The alternative for returning to Christchurch is
Lewis Pass.) The road is surrounded by rugged snow-capped
mountains with dense beech forests to the snowlines and deep
glacially-carved gorges. Follow Bealey Valley and the Bealey
River into the township of Arthur's Pass. The few miles
before the village, Top of the Pass, are well worth walking to
get the most out of the great mountain scenery.

Allow four hours for driving from Greymouth to
Christchurch and the rest of the day for sightseeing activities.
Stop at the Park Visitor Centre, open seven days 8:00 a.m. to
5:00 p.m. (tel. Arthur's Pass 500) in Arthur's Pass village for
information, brochures, detailed maps and to see a variety of
fascinating exhibits on the history, flora and fauna, geology
and other background including an audiovisual presentation
on the building of Highway 73. Just a short walk from the
Visitor Centre is the Devil's Punchbowl Trail to the nearby
Devil's Punchbowl waterfall pouring down a 400-foot gorge.
The Bridal Veil Nature Walk to a view of Bealey Valley from
the Bridal Veil Lookout, about an hour, starts near the Bealey
footbridge. Another one-hour walk from the village, starting
opposite the Dobson Memorial, winds through flower beds
along Dobson Nature Walk.

From Arthur's Pass to Bealey, follow the mighty
Waimakariri River within Arthur's Pass National Park. Watch
for clearly signposted walking tracks, picnic shelters and
camping sites. The Waimakariri River and parallel Highway
73 curve around the northern end of the tree-covered
Craigieburn Range which becomes bare, eroded hills around
the trout-filled Lakes Grasmere and Pearson; changing again
to the beech-covered Craigieburn Forest Park; and yet again
from smooth round hills near Castle to a rather desolate
descent from the 3,000-foot level around Porters Pass to the
fertile Canterbury Plains.

Itinerary options

Returning to Christchurch, you have a choice between
Arthur's Pass (Highway 73) and Lewis Pass (Highway 7).
The west side of Arthur's Pass is especially lush and beautiful.

The Lewis Pass road does not offer the scenic grandeur of Arthur's Pass National Park but does open up worthwhile side-trips—to Hamner Springs, for example. Just west of Lewis Pass is Maruia Springs, hot pools in an alpine setting. In midwinter, Lewis Pass may be easier to cross than Arthur's Pass.

For those returning to the North Island on the Inter-Island Ferry, it's a four-hour drive from Westport to Picton, passing through the very scenic Lower Buller Gorge on Highway 6. This route opens up these options:

Coaltown Trust Museum displays the history of Westport, the country's main coal shipping port.

The Pancake Rocks and Punakaiki Blowholes at Punakaiki Scenic Reserve jut into the sea midway between Westport and Greymouth, stratified rock formations in lush greenery interlaced with rocky grottoes and blowholes.

Consider a side-trip to the Abel Tasman National Park or the Nelson Lakes National Park.

For those wanting to stay overnight, the **Sir Arthur Dudley Dobson Memorial Youth Hostel** in Arthur's Pass Village (tel. AHP 528) has dormitory beds at NZ$8 (£3.20) per person, and the **Alpine Motel** (tel. AHP 583) on the highway has units from NZ$30 (£12) double. The **Store and Tearooms** and the **Chalet Restaurant** in the village can take care of your lunch needs.

TOUR 22

CHRISTCHURCH—BANKS PENINSULA

Take an all-day trip to the unique Banks Peninsula and
Akaroa, a charming village with French atmosphere.
Afterwards, return to Christchurch to relax and enjoy a
special evening.

Suggested schedule

7:00 a.m.	Leisurely breakfast.
8:30 a.m.	Leave for all-day trip to Banks Peninsula and Akaroa.
2:00 p.m.	Visit Okains Bay.
4:30 p.m.	Drop off your car if you have an early morning flight.
	Return to Christchurch for a celebration dinner.

Driving to Akaroa

There are two ways to Banks Peninsula from Christchurch: to
Lyttelton through the road tunnel under Port Hills, past
many beaches and bays (Corsair, Governors Bay, Charteris
Bay, Camp Bay and others), up and down the hills to Port
Levy and Pigeon Bay; and the more usual route via Summit
Road. Take Summit Road for views stretching from Pegasus
Bay to the Southern Alps and out across Banks Peninsula.
Take the road through Sumner, climb Evans Pass across
Bridle Path to the Sign of the Kiwi, where the road between
Governors Bay and Christchurch crosses. Go straight ahead
along Summit Road to Gebbie's Pass and Evans Pass. Follow
State Highway 75 to Birdlings Flat, skirt Lake Forsyth and
continue through Little River over the hills to Akaroa
Harbour. Return to Christchurch on the road through
Taitapu and Halswell, staying on Highway 75 past the
turn-off to the Pass.

If you have an early morning flight tomorrow, drop off
your hired car tonight before dinner, saving time in the
morning. But if you decide to drop it off in the morning,
most hire car companies will drive you to the airport.

Sightseeing highlights

●●●**The Banks Peninsula** is geologically as well as

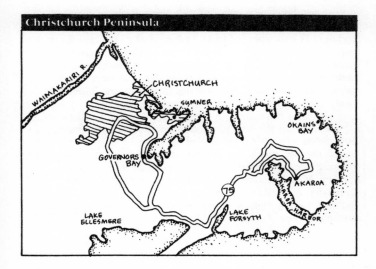

geographically set apart from its Canterbury surroundings. Formed by two extinct volcanoes, the peninsula is cut deeply by narrow bays reached by steep roads off Highway 75. Akaroa is the closest that the French came to colonising New Zealand. In fact, it's just an accident of history that Christchurch is very English rather than Gallic. In 1835, Jean Langlois sailed the whaling ship *Cachalot* into what today is French Bay at the site of Akaroa, sheltered from cold southerly winds. He managed to buy land from the Maoris, returned to France and organised colonists, and left France in March 1840 on the *Comte de Paris*. Britain annexed New Zealand on February 6, 1840. *Mon Dieu!* But at least Jean and the descendents of this frustrated French contingent, resting in the old French cemetery on L'Aube Hill, left their indelible imprint on Akaroa. Many street names and signs are in French. The Langlois Eteveneaux House (1845), at the rear of which is a colonial museum, has been restored by the New Zealand Historic Places Trust. A walking tour should also include visits to St. Patricks (1864) and St. Peters (1863), the domain and views from side streets on surrounding hills above the harbour.

This last day is designed for easy strolling and soaking up atmosphere in a unique, small seaside town with the appearance of a late-Victorian colonial village and a distinct get-away-from-it-all atmosphere. Just savour the relaxation after more than 1,500 miles of travelling. Perhaps dangle a fishing line from the wharf, or take a launch trip in the harbour. If you want information on what to see and do in the town, stop at the Information Centre on the waterfront opposite the wharf. On the way back to Christchurch, in the same spirit visit the village of Okains Bay on the north-east side of the peninsula, just 12 miles from Akaroa. There are lovely scenic walks to explore around the bay, an unpretentious museum in a cottage, stables and a smithy with a Maori section for artefacts found on the peninsula, open daily 10:00 a.m. to 5:00 p.m. (tel. 485).

End the day soaking in a hot bath, reflecting on the trip and thinking about a superb dinner to celebrate a marvellous holiday. May I recommend a suitable last dining treat at **Grimsby's,** corner of Montreal and Kilmore Streets, tel. 799-040, for the right atmosphere and cuisine on your final evening in New Zealand.